KEYS *to* FINANCIAL FREEDOM

STRATEGIES FOR DEBT-FREE LIVING

by

Dennis Leonard

Unless otherwise indicated, all Scripture quotations are from the authorized King James Version.

KEYS TO FINANCIAL FREEDOM: Strategies for Debt-Free Living

Dennis Leonard
9495 East Florida Avenue
Denver, CO 80247
(303) 369-8514
www.dennisleonardministries.com

ISBN 1-880809-20-6
Printed in the United States of America
© 2003 by Dennis Leonard

Legacy Publishers International
1301 South Clinton Street
Denver, CO 80247
www.legacypublishersinternational.com

Cover design by: Chris Gilbert, UDG DesignWorks
www.udgdesignworks.com

1 2 3 4 5 6 7 8 9 10 11 / 09 08 07 06 05 04 03

DEDICATION

This book is dedicated to all who are in search of financial freedom—to those who need a breakthrough in their finances and a change in their life.

Know that God wants to prosper you—with wealth as well as in health, joy, and peace. It's time to follow God's plan for prosperity and unlock your financial future!

> *It shall come to pass, if thou shalt hearken diligently unto the voice of the LORD thy God...all these blessings shall come on thee, and overtake thee* (Deuteronomy 28:1–2).

It's time to believe with me that your best days are still ahead.

ACKNOWLEDGMENTS

I want to thank my wonderful wife, Michele, for her unconditional love, support, and encouragement. With her by my side, I know that I can become all that God has called me to be.

To my sons, Mark and Garret, I want to say how grateful I am to the Lord that you have chosen to use your God-given talents with me in service to the ministry. Together we can touch a hurting world with the love of Jesus Christ.

To the staff of Heritage Christian Center, thank you for your loyalty and support of the vision that God has given us. You have increased the measure of my life tremendously.

Most important, I want to acknowledge the Lord Jesus Christ in all my ways, for it is He who has directed my paths and revealed these keys to financial freedom and abundance in Him.

CONTENTS

KEYS TO FINANCIAL FREEDOM

1

DO YOU HAVE THE KEYS?

Do you remember how excited you were as a teenager the first time someone handed you the keys to an automobile and said, "You drive"?

Do you remember what an awesome feeling you had when you put the keys into the door of the first apartment or home you could truly call your own?

Do you ever feel a little frantic when you can't find your keys?

Keys are important. And this book is all about them.

This book is about opening up the windows of heaven so God's blessings can be poured with abundance into your life. This book is about opening up the wonderful realm of financial freedom. It's a book about how to get into the bonus column when it comes to the way in which you handle your money and material possessions.

There's no point in having keys to a car if you don't intend to drive it or if you have no place to go. There's no point in having keys to a home if you don't intend to open the door and walk in and enjoy that home.

The same is true for the keys to financial freedom. There's no reason to have them if you don't want the fullness of God's blessing. So let me ask you, "Do you see yourself as blessed today?"

Do you have all the resources you need to accomplish all that you believe God has called you to be and do in this life?

Or is your life a constant struggle to make ends meet?

Are you "just barely making it"?

You may have a variety of answers to those questions from a loud and enthusiastic "yes" to a whimpering, whispering "no." The really important question to answer, however, is not one related to where you are at today...but where you want to be in the tomorrows of your life.

Do you like where you are financially?

Do you long to be in a better place financially?

Do you *want* more of God's blessings in your life, including His material and financial blessings?

If your answer to *that* question is a strong "YES!" then this book is for you. These keys are for you.

Many Christians today are barely scraping by from paycheck to paycheck when they should be walking in abundance. Why? The answer is simple. Few Christians have prepared themselves to be blessed according to the way the Word of God says they should be blessed. They haven't made themselves "ready" for the blessing that God desires to give them.

What does it mean to be ready? It means to be prepared, equipped, and positioned to act.

Many of the stories of great athletes are stories about a few minutes of victory and a few hours of glory that follow a much longer time of "getting ready." Olympic-caliber athletes train for years in order to be ready when the time comes for the Games. No gold medal has ever been won by a person who hasn't *prepared* in some way to win it.

Do You Have the Keys?

Have you ever heard the old definition of luck as the moment when "preparation meets opportunity"? Many people miss the opportunities that come to them in life because they haven't prepared.

I recently heard a woman interviewed about a successful record she had made. People were calling her an "overnight sensation." The person interviewing her asked her if this was the case, and the singer responded, "I'm an overnight sensation only if you define overnight as singing for twelve years in every place that had a stage and would loan me a microphone."

Preparation is vital.

But the good news of God's Word—actually, the *great* news—is that unlike an athlete or a want-to-be star, you are guaranteed victory in the financial arena of life if you prepare yourself according to God's plan.

The Bible clearly outlines the preparations you need to make in order to be in a position to receive God's highest and best blessings. There's no mystery involved. The strategy is there for all to read and follow.

A Door Set Before You

The apostle Paul wrote to the Corinthians, *"For a great door and effectual is opened unto me"* (1 Corinthians 16:9).

That is God's message to you and me today.

God's Word shows us the door that He intends for us to walk through. It's a *great* door. There's never anything meager, miserly, or miserable about God's plan. The door He has intended for your life is a door that will fulfill you, satisfy you, enlarge your life, and bring you a *great* blessing.

God's Word tells us repeatedly that God's door for us is an *effectual* door. It's a door that leads somewhere and accomplishes something. It's a door that leads to getting a job done, souls won, and lives improved. God's plan always works and it works to produce an *abundant* life—one marked by God's wholeness in spirit, mind, body, finances, and relationships.

The door of a truly abundant life is set before us. And for many of us, that door remains locked. Most of us aren't living in financial freedom. We aren't living in the fullness of all that we *could* have in

3

our physical health, our mental sharpness, our spiritual power, or our material well-being.

Have you ever seen a door in an apartment or home in a big-city area that has a high crime rate? Some of those doors have four or five locks on them—a series of dead bolts and other kinds of locks. Sometimes it takes several keys to get the door unlocked.

The same is true in our lives. There isn't just one key that unlocks God's *great* and *effectual* door to us. There are a series of keys. But the good news is this...

God's Way Works!

"If folks want to know if God's covenant with us works, the answer from me is a *resounding YES!* I have been a tither for many years now, since 1986 or so, and I would not be where I am today without the Father's faithfulness to me over the years.

"I am a single mom with a grown son who is about to graduate from the Air Force Academy in Colorado Springs, Colorado! I am also an African-American woman, which further attests to the miracle that the Father has done in our lives. I have raised my son through the years by myself with some help from my family, but with no financial or emotional support from the baby's father. In fact, he wanted me to have an abortion but I would not do that.

"I hit rock bottom several years ago now, while attending law school at night and working forty hours during the day-time hours of the week. Every month was a struggle for me to pay rent, keep the utilities on, put food on the table, pay for my car, and keep gas in the car. I was falling further and further behind, and as a result, moved several times from various apartments because of financial difficulties. Then one day when I was tired of struggling, never seeming to get ahead, I cried out to the Lord in my distress. I spent a weekend on my face before Him, saying, 'If You truly raised people from the dead as the Bible says, then show me. I am perishing and I need You. Help me, please!'

"All of a sudden an earthquake hit the area where I lived and when it stopped, the Bible had fallen out of my bookcase. This was the only thing that was disturbed in my apartment. As I picked up that Bible, I knew I was to begin reading it. ***(continued)***

Do You Have the Keys?

God has given us the keys to put into the locks on that **great** *and* **effectual** *door!*

The good news is also...

If we will do our part in putting the keys into the locks. God will open the door for us!

God's Way Works!

"I made a vow to pay my tithe and began paying on it. I also started an in-depth study of the Word on the subject of finances. As I studied the Word, the more I began to learn who the Father really was and how His kingdom works. As my faith grew, coupled with my patient application of it, I slowly began to notice areas of my life beginning to change for the better—or 'prospering' as the Word calls it.

"As the years passed, I got better paying jobs, lived in better apartments, and paid my bills on time. Sometimes I would even have a little extra left over to buy something fun, like a new Bible or a book about the Father's kingdom. Of course, during my times of trial, I didn't have anything that remotely resembled a 'college fund' for my son. Suddenly there he was at eighteen years old, about to graduate from high school, and his mom had no money available to send him to college. Of course, I could have gone into all kinds of debt in order to send him, but the Father came through for us yet again. He received a four-year scholarship to the Air Force Academy! And they even pay him a salary every month for attending there! Now, isn't that just like God?

"I am now buying my dream home and I am establishing my own computer business as the Lord is leading me. Truly the Father is *faithful* and *true* according to His Word.

"Thank you for being the mighty man of valor that you are, Bishop Leonard, and for proclaiming God's Word. Because of your teaching, I am continually strengthened by the Lord to 'continue in the Way.'"

— Sally

By Putting these keys in the
locks and letting God open the
doors for me.

Just turn everything over
to HIm

2

CHOOSE TO DO THINGS GOD'S WAY

Are you satisfied with things in your life? *Fully* satisfied? Is everything just the way you'd really like for it to be? Is that true for your financial life as well as your spiritual, physical, and emotional life?

Most people I know aren't *fully* satisfied. They'd like more or better. They want better health…better relationships with their spouse, children, and friends…a deeper and better walk with God…a promotion at work or an increase in business…a better financial life…and a higher quality of life.

Most people I know are living the way the world says to live. That way can never truly satisfy. And the truth is, the world's way differs from God's way in almost every way!

When someone hurts you, the world says to get even. God says to forgive and let it go.

If you are depressed, the world says to take drugs. God says to praise Him.

When it comes to money, the world teaches you to get all you can and hoard it for yourself. God says to give and you will receive even greater blessings in return.

If you are already doing things the world's way...and that way isn't bringing you all that you desire...it's time to try God's way!

Choose to Believe God's Word

Many Christians have settled for less than God's best for years. In fact, a good percentage of Christians have been taught that God desires for them to live a "simple" life with little or no prosperity. The Bible, however, says the exact opposite!

From the very first chapters of the book we read that God's command to mankind was to have dominion over the earth and to *multiply*. This word *multiply* doesn't mean only that the first man and woman were to multiply by having babies. Rather, the first man and woman were to take a look at everything around them in the Garden of Eden and cause those things—those animals, birds, fish, plants, and all manner of living things—to multiply. They were to be the caretakers and managers of a multiplying process. It was a process of blessing multiplied into blessing multiplied into blessing!

I encourage you to go back and read about the lives of the forefathers of our faith, men such as Abraham, Isaac, and Jacob. We read in a number of places that they had land, cattle, money, and much, much more! God caused them to prosper and multiply.

King David, a man truly in close fellowship with God, was an extremely wealthy, prosperous man. So was his son, Solomon, who was considered to be the wisest man who ever lived.

The Bible presents example after example, command after command, and promise after promise aimed at an *abundance* for God's people, and that abundance includes financial prosperity.

Tell yourself right now, "I believe God's Word. God wants me to be blessed!"

Study and Meditate upon the Word

To truly believe and follow God's way, you must know God's way. You need to study and meditate on God's Word in order to learn all that

8

Choose to Do Things God's Way

God has for you. Knowing God's Word is the foremost thing that will keep your faith alive and energy-filled every waking moment of your life.

The Lord said to Joshua, the great leader of the Israelites after Moses:

> *Be thou strong and very courageous, that thou mayest observe to do according to all the law, which Moses my servant commanded thee: turn not from it to the right hand or to the left, that thou mayest prosper whithersoever thou goest. This book of the law shall not depart out of thy mouth; but thou shalt meditate therein day and night, that thou mayest observe to do according to all that is written therein: for then thou shalt make thy way prosperous, and then thou shalt have good success* (Joshua 1:7–8).

The Lord spoke this to Joshua shortly before Joshua led the Israelites into the Promised Land. These are God's words to you, too, as you get ready to enter into and live in the fullness of all God's promises.

The Lord gave Joshua a two-part formula for good success and prosperity. Part one is courageously keeping the commandments of God. Part two is meditating on God's laws. How can we do that? Here are some practical ways:

Say What God Says. Death and life are in the power of your tongue. What you speak leads you to believe and act in a way that produces either death or life. (See Proverbs 18:21.) As you speak life to yourself, faith rises up in you. As you speak death to yourself, doubt and fear rise up. What does it mean to speak "life" to yourself? It means to speak words of hope, encouragement, appreciation, value, and faith to yourself! The best source of those words is the Bible! Say aloud to yourself God's Word:

- "I am more than a conqueror" (Romans 8:37).

- "God is meeting all of my needs" (Philippians 4:19).

- "Jesus will show me the way because He is the Way" (John 14:6).

9

- "God will bless the work of my hands. His blessings are about to overtake me" (Deuteronomy 28:2,8).

- "In due season I'm going to reap" (Galatians 6:9).

- "I am coming out of financial bondage. I *will* be blessed!"

Every time the children of Israel began to complain and murmur, they experienced great difficulties. Don't be like them! Don't moan about how much you owe or how deep in debt you are. Begin to speak words of faith about how you are going to pay your bills and get out of debt!

Jesus spoke the Word when the devil came to tempt Him in the wilderness. As Christians, we are to follow His example. Stop saying, "I can't get ahead" or "I can't make it." You are just repeating the lies of the devil whispered into your soul. Instead, rise up and say, "I will make it as the Lord helps me!"

I encourage you to memorize Psalm 119:105, which says, *"Thy word is a lamp unto my feet, and a light unto my path."*

Speak God's Word into Your Life. God's Word, spoken into our lives, produces something! The Word is real and powerful. It sets into motion divine principles of God. God spoke through the prophet Isaiah, *"So shall my word be that goeth forth out of my mouth: it shall not return unto me void, but it shall accomplish that which I please, and it shall prosper in the thing whereto I sent it"* (Isaiah 55:11).

God's Way Works!

"**P**astor, you were right...you were right...you were right. Your teaching of God's Word has been manifested in my life. I paid off my creditors one by one and brought my credit report score from 524 to 609. I bought a brand-new house built from the ground up. I sowed seed, paid tithes, worked in the church. I was obedient. And now I have a testimony! Tell everyone, if it can happen to me, it can happen to them, too. I love you. Thank you for your teaching of the Word of God. I pray a wonderful blessing on you." — Donald

Choose to Do Things God's Way

Here are several very practical ways for you to speak God's Word into your life and build up your faith to believe God for financial blessings:

1. Research Scriptures that refer to prosperity and success. Use a concordance or a book of promises to find these verses. As you read your Bible every day, circle or mark passages that relate to money, finances, giving, harvests, or possessions.

2. Write down the verses you find. Writing them out is a way of highlighting them to your own heart and mind.

3. Next to each verse, put a practical implementation idea. Ask yourself, "How can I actually *do* this in my life?" As an idea comes to you, write it down.

4. Insert your name into the scripture. Recognize that this is God's Word to *you*!

5. Turn the verse into a prayer and pray it several times a day. Confess that this verse is true for your life!

Let me give you an example of this. I might find James 1:17 as I research the Bible for verses on giving and receiving. I would write out James 1:17 in my journal:

Every good gift and every perfect gift is from above (James 1:17).

Then next to that verse I might write: "I need to be on the lookout for everything that comes into my life today that I consider to be 'good'—good weather, good driving time to work, good music on the radio, a good meeting with a staff member. I need to praise God for everything I experience that causes a response in me, 'That's perfect!' or 'That's great!' or 'That's awesome!' "

I would insert my name into the verse: "Every good gift to me, Dennis, and every perfect gift to me, Dennis, is from above."

In making this a prayer, I would say to the Lord, "I am trusting You for good gifts and perfect gifts in my life today. I will praise You for every good gift and every perfect gift. Your Word tells me that all good and perfect gifts come from You, so I am expecting good and perfect things from *You*, Lord. I will recognize that any person who is involved in bringing that good thing to my life is Your instrument or vessel of delivery to me."

A prayer like this keeps you looking to God for your harvest, not to other people. It makes you more mindful of the good things God is sending your way every day. It builds an attitude of thankfulness. It points toward blessings. It underscores your need to trust God in all things and to give God praise for all the good that you receive or experience.

6. The final step is to praise God for His manifestations of the verse in your life. In the example of James 1:17 above, God's Word says it's my responsibility to praise Him every time I receive a good word, a good idea, a good gift, a good compliment, a good deed. I need to offer my praise for *all* good!

Watch What You Say to Others. Be careful what you say to others. Don't complain about your bills. Also don't tell people you'll be debt-free in two weeks (unless you are one hundred percent certain you can pay off your bills in that time frame). What you can and should tell people is that you are trusting God and you have a plan for getting out of financial bondage.

When people around you say discouraging words, proclaim the Word of God in response. Tell people they can trust God to turn things around for them.

Speak to Your Bills in Jesus' Name. Pray for God's help in your finances—not that He will take away your bills but that He will help you pay your bills, begin to control your finances, and make wise use of your money. Then, lay hands on your stack of bills and proclaim, "They shall be paid in Jesus' name."

Make a Firm Decision to Obey God's Word. God's Word commands us to keep *all* of His commandments. We don't have the privilege of picking and choosing the ones we want to keep and discarding the rest. God requires obedience to His total plan! It's a little like baking a cake and deciding to leave out a couple of ingredients or substituting an important ingredient with something else...and then still expecting the cake to turn out! If you don't follow the recipe, there's no telling what kind of horrible concoction you might come up with.

God tells us how to achieve blessings. It's up to us to follow His recipe. We must obey Him.

Disobedience is all about *self.* People hate to obey. It goes against what they want. Most people start disobeying as children. They do things behind their parents' backs, knowing that they are disobeying. They develop a rebellious spirit. They don't want to obey their teachers...their bosses...the police...the laws of the land...or anybody in authority over them. Those who live in rebellion reap the harvest of rebellion: failure, disappointment, and a poor relationship with God. Any time a person puts self before God, he cuts himself off from God's blessings.

Obedience is all about doing what *God* says.

Several years after we first started our church, God spoke to my heart about our all-white congregation. He said, "I did not call you to minister to one culture, but to all of My people." I had no idea how much obedience to that command of the Lord would cost me.

We built up a Gospel choir, which was comprised of mostly black people, and we began welcoming all races to our church. We immediately lost several hundred members.

I knew in my heart, however, that I had heard from God and that I was doing what was right before the Lord. We kept doing what we knew was God's commandment. I had a strong belief that God was taking us to a new place and we had to walk in obedience.

It wasn't long before we had more members than ever...and we've been growing ever since.

Obedience comes before blessing. It takes inner strength and courage to choose to keep God's commandments. It takes unwavering commitment, not turning to the left or right but staying on the straight-and-narrow path of obedience. The promise of God that follows obedience is a tremendous one: You will prosper *wherever* you go.

Take Courage! God commanded Joshua to be "very courageous." That means to be bold in your obedience. It means to make a firm decision to walk out God's Word every day of your life.

Renew your commitment to the Lord! Make a decision today...and tomorrow...and tomorrow...and tomorrow that you are going to obey God's Word without wavering. Every day, remind yourself of these truths:

- If I will walk in the ways of the Lord, He will empower me to prosper.

- If I will delight myself in the Word of God, He will establish my life.

- If I will plant my seed, I will see fruit in due season.

- If I will put Him first, I will have wisdom and prosper in everything I do.

Keep the Vision Before You. As you meditate on God's Word, speak God's Word, and pray God's Word into your life, keep your vision about what you are working toward—financial freedom from debt, owning property, the ability to make decisions without financial worry, plans for a business of your own, and wise investments. If you don't have a vision for those things...get one!

Obedience Brings God's Favor

Have you ever met a person who always seems to be in the right place at the right time? Have you ever known a person for whom things always seemed to work out, even when all the odds appeared to be stacked against him?

Did the interest rates go down just at the time he was ready to buy a house? Did she get the job even though she didn't have as much formal education as the other applicants?

That's not luck. That's *favor.*

The Bible tells us that favor is bestowed on those who learn and then obey God's Word. Obedience puts a person into a position to receive favor. Disobedience puts a stop to the flow of favor in a person's life.

The Bible never tells us that a person can pursue a crazy, ungodly lifestyle and then expect God's blessings. It never presents the hope that a person can walk in continual sin, making the same mistakes

14

again and again, year after year, and enjoy the favor of God. Just the opposite! God's favor shines on those who seek to live their lives according to God's commandments.

You may be questioning, "Does that mean I have to be perfect?" No. None of us is perfect, has ever been perfect, or ever will be perfect. We all sin and we all fall short of God's perfect plan for our lives. (See Romans 3:23.)

There's a big difference between being perfect and being obedient. The person who seeks to be obedient is a person who has a heart for following God. Such people's desire is to do what God commands. When they realize they have failed to keep a command of God, they go to God and ask for His forgiveness and for His help in both knowing and keeping the commandments.

Shortly before the children of Israel crossed over into the land God had promised to them—a place God intended for their prosperity—He gave them a stern warning about obedience to His commandments. In one long chapter of the Old Testament, He laid out a choice for the people. (See Deuteronomy 28.) Read God's opening words about this choice:

> It shall come to pass, if thou shalt hearken diligently unto the voice of the LORD thy God, to observe and to do all his commandments which I command thee this day, that the LORD thy God will set thee on high above all nations of the earth: and all these blessings shall come on thee, and overtake thee, if thou shalt hearken unto the voice of the LORD thy God (Deuteronomy 28:1–2).

The chapter goes on for twelve more verses identifying tremendous blessings that represented great prosperity and wealth for God's people. And then we come to the fifteenth verse:

> But it shall come to pass, if thou wilt not hearken unto the voice of the LORD thy God, to observe to do all his commandments and his statutes which I command thee this day; that all these curses shall come upon thee, and overtake thee (Deuteronomy 28:15).

The rest of the chapter—more than fifty more verses!—spell out what will happen to those who do not obey.

The equation is really very simple:

Obedience = prospering abundantly
or
Disobedience = miserable failure

I know one person who saw this distinction so clearly drawn in God's Word and concluded, "It's a no-brainer! Obey!"

Commitment and Determination

It takes commitment and determination to follow God and trust Him with all your life, including your finances. Psalm 1:1–3 speaks about total commitment:

Blessed is the man that walketh not in the counsel of the ungodly, nor standeth in the way of sinners, nor sitteth in the seat of the scornful. But his delight is in the law of the LORD; and in his law doth he meditate day and night. And he shall be like a tree planted by the rivers of water, that bringeth forth his fruit in his season; his leaf also shall not wither; and whatsoever he doeth shall prosper.

Part of the commitment that God calls us to make is a commitment to doing things *His* way, not the world's way. Don't get your financial advice from sinners. Don't turn to those who reject Christ for counsel on what you should buy or how you should make a purchase. Don't go into business with those who are making sin their lifestyle. Choose wise counsel. Choose people who understand and are following the way God has established for prosperity!

Put down deep roots into wisdom. Steep yourself in God's Word. Get all the godly financial teaching you can get. If you'll do that, you will be like a tree. Trees don't usually produce fruit right away. But the good thing about a tree is that it produces more and more fruit over time. The harvest increases and maintains year after year.

The story is told about a farmer who was getting ready to make a big breakfast for some friends. He asked several farm animals what they had to contribute. The chicken quickly volunteered, "I'll give some eggs." She walked proudly back to the other animals. A cow then came forward and said, "I'll give some milk." She returned to the other animals with her head held high. The farmer then turned to look at the pig. "What will you give?" The pig replied, "I will give all that I am."

God is not looking for people who will give just token offerings now and again. He wants a total commitment of your life.

Your empowerment to prosper is tied to your covenant relationship with God. The tithe is part of that covenant. The covenant doesn't depend on your church's style of worship, the preaching style of your pastor, the church music program, or anything else. It depends upon *you* keeping *your* commitment to a holy God. It's about *your* faith and *your* trust in Him. It's about your determination to believe what God declares as truth and to continue to *do* what God tells you to do.

MAKE A COMMITMENT:
"I will do things God's way."

Visit online at www.dennisleonardministries.com.

Doing everything God's way, not my way.

3

SEEK GOD FIRST—
NOT THE BLESSINGS

A very popular line from a movie several years ago was this:
"Show me the money!"

When people talk about God's blessings and God's purposes being
fulfilled in their lives, they very often think that the bottom line is
money. They have a "show-me-the-money" attitude.

God's desire is that we will have an attitude of "Show me the Lord!"
If we truly catch a glimpse of who the Lord is, what the Lord is doing,
and what the Lord desires, we will live in such a way that the money will
come.

It seems to be a sign of our times that people today love their possessions and their pleasures more than they love God. (See 2 Timothy
3:4.) They don't put God first, second, third, or anywhere on their priority list in life. That is, until a crisis happens.

God's challenge to each one of us is to put Him first in all things
all the time.

Is God Really First?

People will do just about anything for money. Or so it seems. Some work. Others steal. Some sell their bodies. Still others sell their souls.

Why? For many people, money represents power. And there is a certain degree of truth in that. Money gives a person the power to go where he wants to go and do what he wants to do.

People also seem to believe that money will bring them self-worth, security, and happiness. Those are *not* true assumptions. Money may buy a person material comfort, but it will not buy joy. Money may produce a certain amount of temporary security, but never lasting security. Money and possessions can disappear quickly, and with the disappearance, there's a great loss of security. Money *never* brings genuine self-worth—it may produce pride, but not genuine self-value.

The truth is that many people who have money feel powerless, insecure, unhappy, and have low self-esteem.

What is money, then, if it is not a sure ticket to a wonderful life? Money simply is a *resource*. It is a purchasing agent. That's *all* it is.

The true source of power, joy, security, and value is a relationship with God. Knowing how to correctly use money and live a life that is fulfilling and satisfying comes only through Jesus Christ. When a person is anchored on the Rock, shifting circumstances and life's storms don't move that person. His joy, his identity, his security, his value remains. If a life is anchored on money, however, everything is in flux because economic situations are always in flux. Stock markets rise and fall. The value of the dollar increases and decreases. Markets undergo inflation and deflation, including the real estate market. There's nothing "sure" about money. Only God changes not—He said through His prophet Malachi, *"I am the LORD, I change not"* (Malachi 3:6). Hebrews 13:8 has the same message: *"Jesus Christ the same yesterday, and to day, and for ever."*

God and Mammon Don't Mix

Jesus taught, *"Seek ye first the kingdom of God, and his righteousness; and all these things shall be added unto you"* (Matthew 6:33). He also said, *"No man can serve two masters: for either he will hate the one, and love the other; or else he will hold to the one, and despise the other. Ye cannot serve God and mammon"* (Matthew 6:24).

That's straightforward talk! Like oil and water, God and the pursuit of money don't mix. You cannot make God and money your top priority at the same time. You either are pursuing God and the riches of the spiritual realm as your top priority, or you are pursuing money and the things of the material and natural realm. There's a choice to be made about what's number one in your life.

God can take care of *all* your needs in a way that exceeds anything you can imagine. He has infinite resources, wisdom, and power at His disposal. He can move heaven and earth to provide what you need. His desire is that we trust Him with all our life—and, in return, He will take care of all our life and provide for us all we need.

If we are pursuing money ahead of God, we are sending a message to God that we don't trust Him to take care of us and lead us into genuine prosperity. Rather, we are relying on our own abilities to earn and manage what comes into our hands.

The issue is one of trust. It's one of dependency. It's one of commitment of our will and submission of our lives.

God promises that if we put Him first, He will cause us to

- Eat the best of the land (Isaiah 1:19)

- Prosper in all we do (Deuteronomy 28:8)

- See everything "added" to our lives that we need or deeply desire (Matthew 6:33).

Who's in Control? Money and issues related to finances have a way of controlling a person's life. How many times have you heard a person who is very concerned about money and the earning or spending of it say things like this: "I can't go to Bible study this Wednesday night because I have to work overtime." "I need to work this Sunday, so I can't make it to church." "I'll give more to God's work as soon as I get the promotion I'm working for." "I know that particular ministry outreach of the church is important, but I just don't have the money right now—I'm investing everything I have in my business." "I realize it's important to spend time in prayer, but I just don't have time right now—I'm working eighty hours a week."

God isn't opposed to our working, having good careers, or building businesses. What He asks of us is that we put Him *first* in our minds, our hearts, our time, and our priorities. When we bring our tithes and offerings to the Lord, we are saying that money is not our god. We are saying we want the Lord and His will more than we crave a new suit, a new house, or anything else in the material realm.

Put God first. Yield control to Him. Blessings will follow.

Your Heart Follows Your Wallet

Many people have an idea of the material and spiritual realms that is "upside down." They tend to think of the material realm as the true reality—things and money are concrete and tangible and therefore "real." They think of the spiritual realm as some sort of floating, invisible, somewhat imaginary realm. Spiritual feelings are perceived to come and go, while material things are perceived as "lasting." Read what Jesus said about this:

> *Lay not up for yourselves treasures upon earth, where moth and rust doth corrupt, and where thieves break through and steal: but lay up for yourselves treasures in heaven, where neither moth nor rust doth corrupt, and where thieves do not break through nor steal: for where your treasure is, there will your heart be also* (Matthew 6:19–21).

It's the spiritual realm that is the true reality. The material realm is subject to the forces of this world—rot, theft, breakdown, and decay.

God knows that where you plant your resources, your heart will follow. That's one of the reasons I believe He instituted the plan of tithes and offerings. What you do with your money speaks volumes about where you put your hope and trust. When you are obedient in giving into God's kingdom, your heart follows. You *value* the Lord and His work far more. You want to be more involved in expanding *His* kingdom, not your own little kingdom.

Submit Your Whole Life Fully to God

Part of being subject to God is resisting the devil. God's promise is that the devil must flee from you if you resist him. James 4:7 tells us, *"Resist the devil, and he will flee from you."* Now this does not mean that you can do your own thing and live any way you want to live and then when troubles come, speak to the devil, "I rebuke you, devil. You have to flee." No! The *first* part of James 4:7 is this: *"Submit yourselves therefore to God."* If you aren't submitting your life to God, your words to the devil have no effect. The devil will laugh at you as he beats you silly!

The apostle Paul wrote to the Corinthians, *"Ye are the temple of the living God; as God hath said, I will dwell in them, and walk in them; and I will be their God, and they shall be my people. Wherefore come out from among them, and be ye separate, saith the Lord, and touch not the unclean thing; and I will receive you"* (2 Corinthians 6:16–17).

Paul was referring to the Corinthians participating in Greek temples that had idols. He said to the Christians in Corinth, *"Be ye separate"* from all that. Don't touch those idols or participate in those things that do not honor the Lord Jesus.

In our world today, this means cutting off your alliances with worldly things and ungodly people. It means you must stop going places that would cause you to compromise your testimony in the Lord. There are places where you should no longer go as a Christian! If you have any doubts about what those places may be, ask your pastor.

The apostle Paul also wrote to the Christians in Ephesus, *"Neither give place to the devil"* (Ephesians 4:27). In other words, don't give the devil even a closet in the home of your soul. Don't give him a hook to hang his hat on! Rather, kick sin out of your house.

It's time for some people to say, "No wed, no bed."

It's time for some people to turn off the TV psychic.

It's time for some people to flush those drugs down the toilet or pour that alcohol down the drain.

Give up any area that you know is a "gray area of sin." If you suspect it's sin, assume that it is! Give it up.

If you truly want a breakthrough in your life, you may first need to have a breakup with that person you know is wrong for you as a business partner, a boyfriend or girlfriend, or a close friend.

The great prayer of Jesus is a prayer we each are called to make our own: *"Not my will, but thine, be done"* (Luke 22:42.)

God's will may seem tough to you. It may seem demanding. Think of it in terms of blessing. Do you want God's blessing? Do you want God's abundance? Then you need to line up your thinking, your attitude, your believing, and your behavior with God's way and God's will.

You can't live any way you want and then say, "But I believe," and expect everything to turn for the better in your life. What you believe and what you do need to line up!

If you get on a roller coaster at an amusement park, the attendant of the ride is likely to tell you, "Don't stand up. Don't push that bar away from you. Don't twist to the left or the right. And you'll make it to the end of the ride." God says to us, "If you will obey Me and don't turn to the left or right, you will make it to the other side." (See Deuteronomy 5:32.) God's other side is a land of promise. It's a land of abundance. It's a land of spiritual strength and financial freedom!

The Lord spoke through His prophet Malachi strong words about putting Him first in our lives:

> *If ye will not hear, and if ye will not lay it to heart, to give glory unto my name, saith the LORD of hosts, I will even send a curse upon you, and I will curse your blessings: yea, I have cursed them already, because ye do not lay it to heart* (Malachi 2:2).

That isn't something I want to experience! That isn't something I want to hear God say in my life!

First in Your Finances, Too! You can't truly put God first in your life until and unless you are willing to put God first in your finances. Too many Christians say, "Well, I don't tithe, but God knows my heart." Yes, indeed! He knows that He doesn't have your heart!

God doesn't want your money or your personal possessions because those things bring Him pleasure. He wants *you*. It's your love and faith and trust in Him that He values. He wants your devotion and your friendship. Tithing is an outward and visible expression that you truly do love Him enough to obey what He commands, that you trust Him enough to give, that you are yielded to Him as a *first* priority. The tithe connects you to the Lord in a supernatural way.

Not long ago a woman asked me to pray for her. Her husband was out of work and they were on the verge of losing their home. I asked her if she tithed. She said, "Well, to be honest, not like I should." In other words, she was saying "no." Either you are tithing or you aren't tithing.

I have to admit that I find it very hard to pray for prosperity or financial blessing for a person if I know that person isn't tithing. All I can truly pray for is God's mercy and God's conviction that a person will come into full obedience to Him. If a person *is* a tither, I can hardly wait to pray for his or her blessing. I know it's coming!

When God is the Lord of your life, you want to do all that He commands. You follow Him with joy! You trust and believe that He is your shepherd, guiding you and directing you into a place of tremendous provision. One of the most famous passages in all the Bible is Psalm 23. It begins, *"The LORD is my shepherd."* And how does that verse end? *"I shall not want."* (See Psalm 23:1.)

God's strategy calls for us to put Him first—to make Him your shepherd. Follow Him as your shepherd. The promise to you is that if you will do this, you *shall not want.*

MAKE A COMMITMENT:
**"God will be Number One in my life.
I will seek Him *first*."**

4

BLESSING OR CURSE?
IT'S A MATTER OF OBEDIENCE

One time when I was preaching a series on financial blessing, a woman came up to me after the first sermon and said, "Bishop Leonard, I waited all night for you to get to the part about giving and receiving. All you talked about was obeying."

I said, "Sister, giving and receiving isn't the real issue. The real issue is obeying or disobeying."

You can make a decision and commitment to give—yes, you can even give—without having a heart to obey. *But...*you cannot make a decision and commitment to obeying God without giving, and you cannot give out of obedience and faith without receiving. If you're going to haul a blessing to market, you need to get the horse before the cart!

I want you to read the following two passages from the Bible *aloud to yourself:*

Passage #1:

And it shall come to pass, if thou shalt hearken diligently unto the voice of the LORD thy God, to observe and to do all his commandments which I command thee this day, that the LORD thy God will set thee on high above all nations of the earth: and all these blessings shall come on thee, and overtake thee, if thou shalt hearken unto the voice of the LORD thy God. Blessed shalt thou be in the city, and blessed shalt thou be in the field. Blessed shall be the fruit of thy body, and the fruit of thy ground, and the fruit of thy cattle, the increase of thy kine, and the flocks of thy sheep. Blessed shall be thy basket and thy store. Blessed shalt thou be when thou comest in, and blessed shalt thou be when thou goest out. The LORD shall cause thine enemies that rise up against thee to be smitten before thy face: they shall come out against thee one way, and flee before thee seven ways. The LORD shall command the blessing upon thee in thy storehouses, and in all that thou settest thine hand unto; and he shall bless thee in the land which the LORD thy God giveth thee (Deuteronomy 28:1–8).

Passage #2:

But it shall come to pass, if thou wilt not hearken unto the voice of the LORD thy God, to observe to do all his commandments and his statutes which I command thee this day; that all these curses shall come upon thee, and overtake thee: Cursed shalt thou be in the city, and cursed shalt thou be in the field. Cursed shall be thy basket and thy store. Cursed shall be the fruit of thy body, and the fruit of thy land, the increase of thy kine, and the flocks of thy sheep. Cursed shalt thou be when thou comest in, and cursed shalt thou be when thou goest out (Deuteronomy 28:15–19).

Now let me ask you:

- How did you feel as you read each of these passages? Did you feel an enthusiasm and optimism as you read the first passage? Did you feel discouraged or "down" as you read the second passage?

28

Blessing or Curse? It's a Matter of Obedience

- Which of these two passages of scripture best describes your life? Are you blessed in *everything* you do? Or are you broke, busted, and disgusted?

Getting Free from the Curse

The Bible is very clear on the fact that there is a curse on this world. That curse started in the Garden of Eden. It continues to this day. The ultimate curse is the curse of spiritual death, but the curse isn't limited to that. The curse includes sickness, poverty, and endless troubles. It includes the division of families and wasted resources. The curse destroys hopes and kills dreams. The curse is the domain of the devil.

The Bible is also clear that freedom from this curse is possible! Jesus Christ came to give us life, and a life that is more abundant (John 10:10). When we trust Him as our Savior and give our life to Him, He redeems us from the curse of spiritual death. His death on the cross paid the price for sin and bought us out of slavery and bondage to sin. As we commit our life to Him and put Him first in everything—truly making Him the *Lord* of our lives—His blessings follow after us and overtake us.

Let me make it very clear:

The Curse of the Devil	The Blessings of Christ
Spiritual death	Spiritual life...eternal life
Sickness and disease	Health and wholeness
Hate, anger, and rebellion	Love
Discouragement and depression	Joy
Frustration, worry, and fear	Peace
Poverty	Prosperity
Divorce, separation, division	Unity in families and friendships
Despair and futility	Hopes and dreams

Which way do you want to live? What is your heart's desire?

Every person I know would choose to live on the "Blessings of Christ" side!

What is the condition God places as a deciding factor about how a person will live? Read again the opening line of Passage #1: *"And it shall come to pass, if thou shalt hearken diligently unto the voice of the LORD thy God, to observe and to do all his commandments"* (Deuteronomy 8:1).

Hearing God's commandments and then observing and keeping God's commandments—that's the two-part condition placed on us if we are to live a life of blessing!

Making the Right Choice

What does it mean to *"hearken diligently"* to the voice of God? It means to seek out the voice of God.

God doesn't speak haphazardly. He doesn't speak from heaven through a huge megaphone. If a person is going to hear the voice of God, he must *seek* to hear the voice of God. He must go where God's Word is being proclaimed. He must go the Scriptures. He must make an effort to hear.

The number one choice that we must make is a choice to put God first and to diligently seek Him and diligently seek to hear His voice. If you truly put the Lord first, nothing can keep you from blessings. They are yours!

People may not like you...but they won't be able to resist blessing you.

Circumstances may line up against you...but they won't be able to defeat you or to stop the flow of God's blessings.

People may reject you, criticize you, or do their best to harm your reputation...but they won't be able to overcome the blessings of God in your life.

If you are in right position with God, nothing...nothing, nothing, absolutely nothing...can keep you from being blessed. The only way you can find yourself in the "cursed" column of life is if *you choose to disobey God.* The devil knows this. That's why he spends so much time and effort to try to tempt you to disobey. That's why he does his utmost to get you to make bad choices when it comes to obeying God's commandments. That's why he does whatever he can to keep you from seeking after God.

Think back over the parable of the prodigal son, which might also be called the parable of the loving father. Jesus told the story of a young man who demanded his inheritance from his father before the father's death, then took that inheritance and squandered it. If you read this parable closely you will see that this young man, as rebellious and jealous as he was, didn't get into trouble until he left the covering of his father. Once he walked away from his father's household, he suddenly was on the devil's turf. When the boy left home, trouble hounded him and camped on his doorstep. He ended up having a "doorstep" that was among the pigs!

When this boy in the parable came to his right spiritual senses and returned home to his father, he again put himself under the covering of his father. There he received blessings—a full restoration of his role as a son, a full provision and protection. (See Luke 15:11–32.)

This parable, of course, is about our relationship with our heavenly Father. Jesus made it very clear that as long as we are in an obedient relationship with God the Father, we experience the fullness of the Father's blessings. It's when we willfully choose to walk away in disobedience that we experience the curse of the devil. As long as we are in close, obedient, and faithful relationship with the Lord, the devil can't touch us.

I had a person tell me just recently that a "witch" had put a curse on her and her family. Let me assure you today, no witch of any kind has any power over you if you are trusting the Lord and are walking in obedience to Him. The devil can launch all kinds of fiery darts against you...but they cannot penetrate your life and do eternal damage to you if you are obeying God's Word and trusting the Lord with all your heart, soul, mind, and strength.

Can you begin to understand why the devil will try to keep a person from attending church? Can you see why the devil will try to keep a person from opening his Bible, stop him from getting on his knees to pray, and stop him from putting his tithe into the offering plate? If you stop obeying the Lord—if you stop seeking Him and stop seeking to hear His voice—you open yourself up to direct assault from the devil. You open yourself up to a life marked by curse, not blessing.

The choice is yours! The Bible makes it very clear: *"I call heaven and earth to record this day against you, that I have set before you life and death, blessing and cursing: therefore choose life, that both thou and thy seed may live: that thou mayest love the LORD thy God, and that thou mayest obey his voice, and that thou mayest cleave unto him: for he is thy life, and the length of thy days: that thou mayest dwell in the land [of promise]"* (Deuteronomy 30:19–20).

If you put God first and foremost in all things, you succeed.

If you put anything before God, everything you touch will ultimately fail.

It's just that clear-cut.

Not Easy. It's not easy to make right choices. There's a price to pay for obedience. Every day can seem like a test. You may find that everything seems to go wrong when you start walking right. The good news is that God walks through the testing times with you. He gives you strength as you make right choices. He turns things around, and ultimately, if you put all your life in God's hands, He causes you to experience blessing.

Obeying God's Statutes

God's Word declares that blessings are ours if we *"observe"* and *"do"* all the commandments of God. At times, the Bible talks about obeying God's statutes.

What is the difference between a commandment and a statute? In technical terms, a commandment is a statement of overriding principle and law. A statute is a "rule" that is very practical, very direct.

The Ten Commandments are just the opening commandments about how God expects us to order our lives. (See Exodus 20:1–17.) The first four of the commandments spell out our relationship with God. We are to put God first, have no idols, refrain from taking the Lord's name in vain, and keep the Sabbath. The next six commandments spell out our relationship with other people. We are to honor our parents. We must not kill, commit adultery, steal, bear false witness against our neighbor, or covet our neighbor's possessions.

Jesus taught: *"Thou shalt love the Lord thy God with all thy heart, and with all thy soul, and with all thy mind. This is the first and great commandment. And the second is like unto it, Thou shalt love thy neighbour as thyself. On these two commandments hang all the law and the prophets"* (Matthew 22:37–40).

The Ten Commandments, and all of the other commandments, point us to the two "great commandments" taught by Jesus. They tell us how to love God with our whole heart, soul, and mind. They tell us how to love others.

If you want to know God's will for your life, start with the commandments!

"But what about the statutes?" you may be asking.

The statutes were also commandments. God ordained them and authorized their keeping from generation to generation. They were the practical rules that were to govern a righteous person's life. Paying the tithe and giving offerings are part of the statutes. (See Malachi 3:10.)

Throughout the Bible, we find repeated passages that point us to the truth that if a person doesn't put the Lord first in his life—if he doesn't "love God with heart, soul, and mind," he is in disobedience. He isn't keeping the first commandment.

We find throughout the Bible passages that point to the truth of the second great commandment. If a person doesn't love others as himself, he is in disobedience.

We also find passages that point to the great importance of keeping the statutes or the practical commandments. The statutes give us concrete and specific ways of determining if we are in a loving relationship with God and other people.

The tithe, for example, is a very concrete and specific statute that lets us know if we are truly loving God and faithfully seeking to obey Him.

The Reason for a Curse

God doesn't allow a curse in your life because He's mad at you. The truth is that He loves you enough to get your attention and try to get you to change you mind. The purpose of the "curse" is to get you to make a change in your life and to choose obedience!

"How can I tell if my finances are cursed?" you may ask.

A curse often displays itself in these kinds of ways:

- You can never get ahead. You live from paycheck to paycheck and never seem to have anything when an emergency comes along.

- You find that you frequently look at other people and say, "They seem so lucky" because they are able to afford things you can't afford—even though they work where you work and make about the same amount of money you make.

- Your roof springs a leak, the car breaks down, and the dog runs away...and you wring your hands and complain, "Why me?"

If you confess to being a Christian and claim to love God but you frequently make excuses about obeying "certain parts" of the Bible...you are living under a curse.

If you find that you are continually questioning why you are broke...you are experiencing a curse.

If you find that you have a great feeling of dissatisfaction all the time about money and bills and your financial future...you are living under a curse.

Generational Curses on Finances. Some of the financial curses we experience have been passed down to us. Daddy didn't know how to manage money and wasn't a tither because his daddy didn't know how to manage money and wasn't a tither...and therefore, we don't know how to manage money and aren't tithing. There are a number of generational curses that we see all around us.

Abusive behavior can be such a curse. Depression, feelings of dejection, and low self-value can be such a curse. Poverty can be such a curse.

There are some families in which poverty seems to have become a way of life—even to the point where the people who are living in poverty can't even imagine a life that isn't marked by poverty. They've lived on welfare so long they can't imagine getting off welfare. They've lived in the tenements for so many generations they can't imagine living in any other neighborhood.

Just because the curse is generational doesn't mean it's not painful. Just because your family has been living "on hard times" for a long time and everybody in your family is in that same "poor boat" doesn't mean hard times and poverty are enjoyable. No! If you have ever visited a prison, you know that prisoners live a hopeless life, especially those who are in for very long sentences or who are in for "life without parole." Generational poverty is like living in such a prison.

It's up to each one of us to break *free* from these generational curses on our lives. It's up to us to break free of the curse in the name of Jesus!

Close the Loophole to Reverse the Curse

You may love the Lord but if you don't give God the firstfruits as He commands, then the devil has a legal open window through which to steal from you. You've created a loophole for a curse.

The Bible says the devil prowls about like a lion, seeking the easy target: *"Be sober, be vigilant; because your adversary the devil, as a roaring lion, walketh about, seeking whom he may devour"* (1 Peter 5:8). If you give the devil an opportunity, he'll take it. The devil doesn't have an ounce of mercy in him. If he sees an opportunity to steal your money through sickness, bad jobs, malfunctioning cars and appliances, lost investment opportunities, or in any other way, he'll pounce on that opportunity and rob you of as much as he can. In the process, he'll steal your joy, your peace, and your relationships.

Look closely at what God's Word says in Malachi 3:8–9:

> *Will a man rob God? Yet ye have robbed me. But ye say, Wherein have we robbed thee? In tithes and offerings. Ye re cursed with a curse: for ye have robbed me, even this whole nation.*

The Bible doesn't say God curses you when you don't tithe. Neither does it say that the devil curses you. You curse yourself! You are the one who, through your disobedience, puts yourself under a curse. Once you are there, the devil just walks through the legal loophole you've created. He comes right through that open window into your life and creates as much havoc as he can.

There's a "double whammy" that occurs when a person who is part of the family of God doesn't tithe. First, that person is in a position of stealing from God—he diminishes God's work in the midst of the church.

Second, the person opens the door of his life to satanic attack. He, in essence, robs himself. We all know people who just cannot seem to get ahead. They work, but the company that hired them folds or they get "downsized" right out of a job. They get some money, but it seems to flow right through their hands like water. They are living under a financial curse. They have opened the door to satanic attack in their lives and they are in a position to be ripped off continually by the devil.

God has a different plan for His people, and if His people will follow it, they can reverse this curse. The curse isn't reversed because His people start handling their money better or because they get a better job. The curse is reversed when God's people begin to have enough faith to bring God their tithes and offerings. The minute a person begins to walk in obedience by giving tithes to the Lord with a heart that is trusting Him, loving Him, and desiring to serve Him...God slams shut that open window into your house. He cinches off the loophole the devil has been crawling through. He puts handcuffs on the devil and says, "Don't go here. This person is Mine."

Tithing puts you out of the "destined to fail" category and into the "destined to succeed" category! The giving of the tithe is the entry point into the fullness of God's blessings.

MAKE A COMMITMENT:
"I will obey! I will keep *all* God's commandments."

Visit online at www.dennisleonardministries.com.

5

THE CORNERSTONE OF GIVING: THE TITHE

When we think of a cornerstone of a building in our modern world, we tend to think of a commemorative plaque placed on the corner of a building—the place where perhaps the name of the building, the architect's name, the year of construction, and other pieces of information are engraved.

That isn't what a cornerstone was in ancient times.

In Bible times, buildings were often cut into a hillside, at least in part. On the side of the building opposite the hill—in other words, the less steep side of the building—a large stone was placed. This stone created a point of strength to balance the downward gravity of the hillside. The stone was hewn to be something of an "L" shape so that the walls could be built in ninety-degree angles on this stone in the corner.

Some of these ancient cornerstones actually appear heart-shaped—the "L" is thick on both sides, yet not a perfect square.

Why is this concept important to us when it comes to our giving? Three reasons. First, there's a "downhill" force that works against many of us in our financial life. Problems, tragedies, and general desires and wants of life put a pressure on our giving. The person who is not truly committed to giving to the Lord will find dozens of other "needs" that tug at his wallet. He'll find all sorts of things that need purchasing or need paying.

Second, if a person tries to build a wall opposite a hillside by putting stones on top of one another in an unspecified pattern, that wall will have no strength. It has no "resisting" power to the downhill gravity of the opposite side of the structure. The same is true in our giving. If a person just gives "at random," a little here and a little there like a stone on top of a stone, unconnected in time and location, that giving is unproductive. Over time, that wall won't be completed...it won't stand...it won't be strong. On the other hand, if giving has a cornerstone that is strong and sure, giving is coordinated and layered in such a way that it truly produces the desired effect...the desired wall of strength...the desired result.

Third, our giving is to flow from our love for God. Giving isn't a gimmick. It isn't a fad scheme. Giving is the response we should have to God's love poured out to us. Giving should be reflected in our outstretched arms to the world—like the two sides of an L-shaped stone, our heart of love reaches out from us toward those in need and those who don't know the Lord.

Our motivation for giving must be a love for God and a desire to obey Him. We must give with a desire to experience spiritual strength and enduring productivity. We must give with a loving concern for the Lord's work and people in need—a heart filled with love that overflows into very practical projects and ministries. The result of building on a cornerstone is a *wall*. When we give on the cornerstone provided in the Bible, the wall we build in the spirit realm is a wall of prosperity.

The Tithe Is the Cornerstone

So what is the cornerstone for our giving? It is the tithe. God commands us to tithe. It is the first and foremost key that unlocks God's blessings. The Lord said through the prophet Malachi:

The Cornerstone of Giving: The Tithe

Bring ye all the tithes into the storehouse, that there may be meat in mine house, and prove me now herewith, saith the LORD of hosts, if I will not open you the windows of heaven, and pour you out a blessing, that there shall not be room enough to receive it. And I will rebuke the devourer for your sakes, and he shall not destroy the fruits of your ground; neither shall your vine cast her fruit before the time in the field, saith the LORD of hosts (Malachi 3:10–11).

God knows how we humans think. He knows that the vast majority of people are long on intention and short on action—long on "heart feelings" and short on committed action. He knew we would have a difficult time putting Him first when it comes to our money, so He implemented the "firstfruits plan." The tithe is intended by God to be the *first* tenth that we give. Very specifically, the tithe refers to the number ten. We are to take the *first* ten percent of our income and give it to God.

Giving is not a natural-born instinct. Even as young children, we fight for what we think is "ours." One of the first words a child learns is "mine!" And even before the child learns the word, he has the instinct to cling tightly and not let go of things he wants and that he intuitively believes are his right to hold.

Giving is an act of surrender—of giving up something that is in our possession. In the spiritual realm, giving is an act of totally surrendering ourselves to God. It is putting ourselves into an "empty vessel" position with the desire that God will fill us and use us as He desires. It is a sign to ourselves as well as to God and others that we are "sold out" to God—we are giving Him not only what is rightfully His, but also what we at times have erroneously thought to be rightfully ours. It is saying to the Lord, "I know and accept the truth that *all* things come from you—my life, my health, my spiritual salvation, my intellect, my abilities, my skills, my job, my children, and *all* my material possessions."

A major misunderstanding that stops people from obeying God in tithing is this: They think the money they give disappears the moment they give it. They think that the money that was in their hands was theirs, and that the moment they release it as a gift to God, that money disappears from their "account."

The exact opposite is true. In the first place, the money in their hands wasn't truly theirs. The tithe belongs to God whether a person gives it or not. It's God's money. It's the firstfruits that He has commanded and appropriated as His. If a person spends the tithe on his own self, he isn't spending his money...he is spending God's money. *All* things come from God and, in truth, all things are God's all the time! He has commanded, however, that we bring the tenth. God generously gives us *all* and then commands that we give back ten percent so He can take that amount and use it *on our behalf.*

The money you give as a tithe is accrued to your account in the spiritual realm. The only difference is that God is your investments broker! He is the One who takes on the responsibility for multiplying that tithe and giving it back to you in a bountiful, overflowing, abounding harvest.

Proverbs 3:9 clearly commands, *"Honour the LORD with thy substance, and with the firstfruits of all thine increase."* That verse is immediately followed by this promise: *"So shall thy barns be filled with plenty, and thy presses shall burst out with new wine"* (Proverbs 3:10). God's response to a person giving the tithe will be one marked by this phrase: *"filled with plenty"*! There will be a "bursting out" of God's blessing!

God's Way Works!

"In November 1998, I decided to become a tither. In February 1999 my father, whom I saw only four times in my life, passed away. His current wife didn't seem to like me when I had visited them, so I did not expect an inheritance. Then we got a letter saying that my father had left an insurance policy and that my sisters and I were to get five thousand dollars each when my father's wife passed away. We thought that was a blessing...but we had no idea what God *really* had in mind. In the settling of my father's estate, the courts determined that his current wife *and* my sister and I were his legal heirs. To our great surprise, we each received a check for $38,000. Money also was given to my children when they graduated from high school. God is a great God!" — Becky

The Cornerstone of Giving: The Tithe

Malachi 3:10–11, quoted earlier in this chapter, clearly says *"bring ye all the tithes into the storehouse."* What are the two results of that? First, there will be meat in God's house. In other words, all of the ministries of the church will be funded. Second, there will be an abundance poured back out on the one who gives. The blessing will be so great *"there shall not be room enough to receive it."* Not only that, but any force that comes against the person's life—to devour his substance, destroy his health, defeat his success, demolish his family—will be rebuked by God. Nothing that is productive or beneficial in a person's life will be cut short—that's what it means when God says the vine will not cast its fruit before the fruit is ripe. Talk about prosperity—a blessing so great it cannot be contained, a rebuking of any destructive force against your life, and total productivity and accomplishment for everything good God commands you to do!

"But does this really work?" you may ask.

The Bible gives story after story of just how wonderfully this principle worked in various lives.

Abraham gave *"tithes of all"* and immediately after that, we read in the Bible that God entered into a covenant with Abraham in which He gave to him *"this land, from the river of Egypt unto the great river, the river Euphrates."* And not only that, but God promised to give the land as a perpetual gift to children Abraham did not yet have! (See Genesis 14:20 and Genesis 15.)

When Jacob left his father's house with nothing but the clothes on his back, he vowed to give God the tithe, saying, *"Of all that thou shalt give me I will surely give the tenth unto thee"* (Genesis 28:22). About twenty years later, Jacob returned to his hometown with such an abundance of flocks, herds, and servants that he sent a token present to his brother Esau of *"two hundred she goats, and twenty he goats, two hundred ewes, and twenty rams, thirty milch camels with their colts, forty kine, and ten bulls, twenty she asses, and ten foals"* (Genesis 32:14–15). Imagine the immensity of Jacob's flocks and herds if he could give a "token gift" of more than five hundred and fifty animals!

I don't know of another investment plan that has that kind of return on a consistent, reliable basis. When you give your money to promote the Gospel of Jesus Christ, God blesses you in return!

Every verse that commands giving in the Bible is given with that underlying promise. Jesus said, *"Give"*...and what were the next words He spoke? *"And it shall be given unto you."* Jesus' promise was also marked by an abundant, abounding overflow. He said,

> *Give, and it shall be given unto you; good measure, pressed down, and shaken together, and running over, shall men give into your bosom. For with the same measure that ye mete withal it shall be measured to you again* (Luke 6:38).

Some people say, "Well, yes. If I give to God, He takes what I give and puts it in a spiritual account and I'll receive a spiritual reward in heaven."

That's not what God's Word says. God's Word is very concrete— Proverbs speaks of barns filled and presses bursting with new wine. Malachi speaks of the fruit of the ground being preserved and a blessing that can't be contained in a tangible way. Jesus said that men shall *"give into your bosom."*

God's Way Works!

"When my wife and I began tithing, it was just because we wanted to obey the Bible. I don't think we really had much expectation for great results. We were okay financially—not too good and not too bad—making it. After faithfully tithing for several yeas, we started to look back over our lives and realized that we had been increasing bit by bit for a long time. We kept getting the best. I received raises on my job even when it was not raise time. Not only that, but money kept coming in from unusual sources. When difficult situations happened, we prayed God's promises in Malachi 3 and asked God to rebuke the devourer for us because we were tithers.

"We had ten thousand dollars worth of medical bills that were paid even though they were initially turned down for payment by our insurance company. We found that one of the biggest blessings was the wisdom that God gave us day by day. Our decisions were blessed by God.

"We believe we are in a blessing cycle. We will never, ever turn back from tithing. It is our goal now to increase our offerings and try to match our offerings to our tithes. God's plan is the only plan as far as we are concerned." — Randy

The Cornerstone of Giving: The Tithe

What did Jesus mean?

Men kept their moneybags tucked into their belted tunics just above the belt—inside the folds of their garment. The moneybag was, therefore, kept in the "bosom" of a man. Jesus was speaking very practically about money. In our terms today, this verse may very well have been translated, "shall men put into your wallet."

God's blessing for giving the tithe—which was a tithe of money and material substance—was a harvest of money and material substance!

You cannot beat God at giving. The return of your giving the tithe to Him is always an overflowing, abounding, multiplied return.

That isn't what the world will tell you...but let me ask you this: Haven't you tried the strategies of this world? With what results? Can you tell me that any of the world's financial systems *guarantees* an abundant return? No! The stock market may rise...but it also falls. Banks pay interest...but banks have been known to fold. Real estate may increase in value...but it also may decrease in value. Money hidden under the mattress doesn't produce any increase.

Are You Giving Your Tithe to God?

One of the basic principles of life is this: If something isn't growing, it's dying. Life is marked by growth, by developing, by forward and upward and onward change. Giving puts us into a position to experience that kind of life, a life Jesus described as life *"more abundantly"* (John 10:10).

Are you giving your tithe regularly, consistently, and cheerfully to God?

If you are, you have established a cornerstone in your life for a *total* life of prosperity, abundance, and ongoing blessing.

If you are *not* tithing, you do not have a cornerstone for genuine prosperity and financial freedom in your life. The plain truth is you, as a *non*-tither, are in disobedience to God's commands. If you are *not* tithing, you are not trusting God with your whole life. You are not fully believing the Gospel. If you are *not* tithing, you have not put yourself into a position to prove the truth of God's Word in your life when it comes to financial blessing. You don't have the most basic and obvious evidence in your life that you are putting God first or

43

that your love for Him is genuine. You have not put yourself into a position to grow spiritually or to produce eternal fruit.

My challenge to you today is to lay a strong cornerstone in your life for financial freedom. Start tithing. Continue tithing. And do so with great joy and faith!

MAKE A COMMITMENT:
"I will obey God—I will give God the tithe He commands me to give."

6

THE BIBLE'S "TOP TEN" TITHING PRINCIPLES

David Letterman, one of the most famous late-night comedians of our day, is famous for his "top ten" lists. Well, I also have a "top ten" list when it comes to tithing. My list is a list of Bible principles. Whereas David Letterman's lists are based on his opinion and are intended to be funny, my list is based upon the absolute Word of God and is of utmost serious importance!

Through the years, I have heard people make all kinds of excuses for not giving the tithe to God's storehouse. I want to say to them, "You don't know what you don't know! You don't know what you are missing out on! You don't know what you're doing to yourself!" The Bible gives us ten major principles related to the tithe. Count them as reasons why you *must* make tithing the cornerstone of your giving.

l. Scripture Commands Us to Tithe

Let me declare this to you today: An excuse for not tithing is an empty excuse. In the end, it is an act of disobedience against God's command, *"Bring ye all the tithes."* Read what God has said:

- *"All the tithe of the land, whether of the seed of the land, or of the fruit of the tree, is the LORD's: it is holy unto the LORD. ...Concerning the tithe of the herd, or of the flock, even of whatsoever passeth under the rod, the tenth shall be holy unto the LORD"* (Leviticus 27:30,32). Wealth in Bible times was calculated in terms of flocks and herds, by acreage of vineyards, olive trees, herbs, wheat, barley, and other produce-yielding and grain-yielding (seed) crops—which is what is meant by *"seed of the land"* and *"fruit of the tree."* Anything that produced "increase" to a person's wealth was to be tithed.

- *"Thou mayest not eat within thy gates the tithe of thy corn, or of thy wine, or of thy oil, or the firstlings of thy herds or of thy flock, nor any of thy vows which thou vowest, nor thy freewill offerings, or heave offerings of thine hand"* (Deuteronomy 12:17). The tithe was to go to the house of the Lord—it was not to be "consumed" by the giver in his own dwelling.

- *"Thou shalt truly tithe all the increase of thy seed, that the field bringeth forth year by year"* (Deuteronomy 14:22). We are to tithe *"all the increase."*

Throughout the Bible, God's people are commanded to give to the Lord the first tenth of all they make.

A Test of Our Obedience. Keeping this commandment to tithe may very well be the most difficult test of your obedience to the Lord. But remember this...because something is difficult does not in any way make it less valid or necessary.

A Strengthener for Our Faith. The truth also is, keeping this difficult commandment may also be the greatest faith-strengthener! God always helps people to do what He requires of them. Trust God to help you obey. The harder it is to tithe and the more you trust God to help you tithe, the more you will experience God's help and the stronger your faith in Him will grow!

2. God Promises to Provide for Those Who Tithe

When you bring your tithe to God's storehouse, He says that He will "open the windows of heaven and pour out a blessing" on you.

The Bible's "Top Ten" Tithing Principles

(See Malachi 3:10–12.) Your tithe triggers the opening of heaven's windows. God's promise is that He *will* take care of those who put their trust in Him. He says that we are to *"prove"* Him in this—it's as if God is saying, "Try it and see. Put Me to the test. Prove whether I'm faithful or not."

Are you willing to take God up on His promise to you?

3. Giving Is the Foundation of the Gospel

Perhaps the most famous verse in all the Bible is John 3:16, which says, *"For God so loved the world, that he gave his only begotten Son, that whosoever believeth in him should not perish, but have everlasting life."* God loved...God gave. The Gospel can be summed up in those two simple phrases. God loved and God gave. God's motivation for giving Jesus to die on the cross was His great love for mankind, including you and me.

God loved us first (1 John 4:19). He didn't love us because we were worthy to be loved. He didn't love us for anything we did, accomplished, or earned. He didn't love us because we had developed a perfect sinless track record. No! God *"commendeth his love toward us, in that, while we were yet sinners, Christ died for us"* (Romans 5:8). God loved us in *spite* of our sin. He loved us because it was His desire, His will, His motivation to love us.

Did God reap from what He sowed? Absolutely! His great reward for giving Jesus as the sinless atoning sacrifice on the cross were the souls of millions of people through the ages.

God set into motion the ultimate display of giving and receiving. What He gave to us is immeasurable and infinite—it is eternal, glorious, and worthy of all praise. In like manner, when we love God, we are compelled to give. It's impossible to love genuinely and fully without giving. Certainly what we give back to God is finite and insignificant—it can never be compared to what God has given to us. Even so, God tells us that when we give to Him, He takes our gift as a sign that we love—a sign that we love to the point of obeying His commandments—and He puts into motion a harvest back to us. He receives and honors our gift, even as He receives and values our love.

4. Giving Proves God's Word Is True

I mentioned earlier that God told us to *"prove"* Him with our giving. The truth is, every time we give, we put God's promises to the test. We verify not only that Malachi 3:10–12 is true, but we also validate all the Bible's promises related to giving.

Have you ever been given a parking-lot ticket with the instructions that if you made a purchase at any of the stores or restaurants in the mall where you were shopping, you could have that parking-lot ticket "validated" and receive free parking? Indeed, when you presented the parking-lot ticket to a clerk or cashier, that person stamped the ticket and as you prepared to exit the parking lot, you were allowed to pass "free" just as was promised to you.

To validate something is to declare it to be "true and in effect." It is to say, "What was promised will come to pass."

God's Word is a little like that parking-lot ticket. His promise to you is that when you give your tithe, you will be given a blessing. As you tithe, you in essence are handing your "ticket" to the Lord. He puts His stamp of approval on your tithe. He says, "I declare that all the promises related to your giving are now fully in effect in your life."

Certainly God's Word is truth at all times. What we do doesn't "make" the principles of God's Word true. But the fact is, many of us don't believe God's principles are true *for us*. We think they may be true in some sort of cosmic, whole-world sense. We think they may be true for other people. But we often don't truly grasp that all of God's principles in his Word are true for us personally and individually. When we give, we are putting ourselves into a position to have God's Word proven as true *for us*.

Time and again people have said to me, "Pastor, I'm receiving my harvest. God's Word is true!" What they are telling me is that they now know from personal experience that God's Word is true in their lives. Are you proving the truth of His Word for *you*?

5. Giving Teaches Us to Put God First

Jesus said, *"Seek ye first the kingdom of God, and his righteousness; and all these things shall be added unto you"* (Matthew

6:33). By *"all these things"* Jesus was referring to food, drink, and clothing. (See Matthew 6:31–32.) Jesus said, *"Your heavenly Father knoweth that ye have need of all these things"* (Matthew 6:32). Jesus was being very practical.

God's Word tells us, *"Thou shalt truly tithe all the increase of thy seed, that the field bringeth forth year by year...**that thou mayest learn to fear the LORD thy God always"*** (Deuteronomy 14:22–23).

The purpose God placed on tithing was that His people would *"learn to fear the LORD...always!"* This didn't mean to be scared of God. To *"fear the Lord"* meant to stay in awe of God and to continually revere His power, majesty, glory, and wisdom. It meant to keep God first in their eyes.

Every time you put your tithe into the offering basket, you are sending a message to your own heart—to your own will, your own mind, your own spirit—"God is first. Obedience to God matters most."

When we refuse to tithe we also are sending a message to our heart—to our will, mind, and spirit—"I don't think it's important to obey God. Self matters most. I'm number one, not God."

It's been said often, "If you want to know a person's priorities, take a look at their checkbook." What you value dictates your spending habits. Ultimately, if God has our finances, He also has our hearts. Visit online at www.dennisleonardministries.com.

6. Giving Is Essential for Spiritual Growth

Jesus said, *"If therefore ye have not been faithful in the unrighteous mammon, who will commit to your trust the true riches?"* (Luke 16:11) Many people want God to bless them tremendously with spiritual gifts—they want to have spiritual power and authority; they want to operate in the gifts of healing and prophecy and faith and miracles. At the same time, they don't want to obey God's commandments, including the ones related to giving. Jesus said very clearly, "If you aren't going to be faithful in keeping the very practical commandments related to your possessions and money, why do you think God is going to entrust to you His spiritual gifts?"

How can you trust God for the intangibles of life if you can't trust Him with the tangibles? How can you trust God to bless you in all the areas of life that are unseen—your health, your happiness and joy, your creativity and energy and vitality, your feelings of fulfillment and satisfaction—if you don't trust Him *first* with your tithes and offerings and the "things" that are visible and concrete?

7. Giving Is Evidence of Your Love for Jesus

Giving is a sign of your love for Jesus Christ.

On the last night before Jesus was crucified, He said to His followers, *"If you love me, keep my commandments"* (John 14:15). He repeated this, saying, *"He that hath my commandments, and keepeth them, he it is that loveth me"* (John 14:21). A third time Jesus

God's Way Works!

"When we first began Heritage Christian Center, we had services in a storefront building. We were barely making it. The rent was hard to meet each month. Then God led me to tithe ten percent of everything that came in to the church. In other words, we 'tithed' as Heritage Christian Center. That seemed impossible to do at the outset because we were sinking fast! But in obedience we gave away food and clothing...we gave time to go into the prisons to minister...we did other things as the Lord directed us. It was a tremendous sacrifice. But within one month we had enough money to cover our expenses and help others. Month by month, God provided and the overflow started to come.

"Soon, we needed a new building. We began a building fund. People worked very hard and, over time, we had about fifty thousand dollars in that fund. We still needed $150,000 more to buy the land we wanted...and that didn't include the building we wanted to put on it.

"A missionary came to our church about that time and God spoke in my heart to give $17,000 to him. It seemed like a lot—and it was. It was money we *needed*, or so we thought, for the land. But God said to give it as a sacrifice and, by faith, we planted it. Within one year, we had what we needed to buy the land for our building. **(continued)** spoke to them and said, *"If a man love me, he will keep my words"* (John 14:23).

And what is it that Jesus commanded? *"Love one another."* But that isn't all Jesus commanded. Jesus didn't limit our love to those who love us or who are committed to Christ. He said we also are to love our enemies. He said we are to *"do good, and lend."* He commanded us to be *"merciful, as your Father also is merciful."* He told us to *"judge not"* and *"condemn not"* so that we might not be judged or condemned. He told us to *"forgive"* so we might be forgiven. And He told us to *"give"* so that we might receive in *"good measure, pressed down, and shaken together."* (See Luke 6:35–38.)

Our giving is a sign of our sincere desire to obey and love the Lord. The apostle Paul took up a monetary collection—an "offering" in our

God's Way Works!

"Every time we have faced a big need, God has led us to plant a big seed. And in planting that seed out of our love and obedience—and with a lot of faith—we have seen God provide an overflow harvest.

"When I first started our church, God led me to go after people who could not help us financially—drug addicts, alcoholics, welfare mothers. We went after those who were down and out. With those very people, God did the miraculous—we were able to pay off a sixteen million-dollar facility within several years after we started building. We didn't have large gifts coming in. The largest one-time gift we ever received was twenty-five-thousand dollars. That's a drop in the bucket compared to sixteen million dollars—a wonderful and encouraging drop but a drop nonetheless! We know it was God who produced this miracle of finances. It came from people obeying and loving and believing and *tithing*.

"We now have given satellite dishes to about twenty-six prisons in our area so we can minister to the prisoners weekly. We service those satellites and pay for their maintenance. The end result is that we have great favor with the government of our state.

"Jesus taught that if you hold tightly to what you have, you'll lose it. But if you give generously—literally turning yourself inside out for God—you'll never stop receiving from Him." — Bishop Dennis Leonard terms today—to help the believers in Jerusalem who were under intense financial persecution. The churches in Macedonia responded eagerly and generously. Paul then wrote to the church in the great Greek city of Corinth, *"Therefore, as ye abound in every thing, in faith, and utterance, and knowledge, and in all diligence, and in your love to us, see that ye abound in this grace also...to prove the sincerity of your love"* (2 Corinthians 8:7–8).

It isn't enough that you know your Bible, have faith, operate in spiritual gifts, and are diligent in your Christian service or ministry to others. It's vital that you abound in this grace of *giving* as well. It's a matter of proof related to the sincerity of all that you profess about loving God and trusting God.

It's proof to others...but first and foremost, it's proof to your own heart and life. It's proof to *you* that you have priorities squared away. It's evidence to you that you truly are in an obedient love relationship with your heavenly Father.

You can say you love the Lord...but actions always speak louder than words. Your obedience in giving will either substantiate or negate the words from your lips, "I love You, Lord."

8. Giving Is an Investment in Eternity

When you give your tithes and offerings to the Lord's work, you are doing something that has eternal benefit.

Jesus said, *"Lay up for yourselves treasures in heaven, where neither moth nor rust doth corrupt, and where thieves do not break through nor steal"* (Matthew 6:20).

An angel of the Lord said to Cornelius, a Gentile in Caesarea, *"Thy prayers and thine alms are come up for a memorial before God"* (Acts 10:4). In other words, God sees and *remembers* your prayers and your acts of giving.

What we give on this earth is recorded...it's remembered...it's "accounted for" in heaven. We are investing in the furtherance of God's kingdom, and ultimately, that kingdom is the heavenly, eternal kingdom.

A gift to the Lord's work is a gift that functions to bring about the salvation of souls, the programs that edify and disciple the saints, programs that spread the Word of God, programs that build up faith. Many of the practical programs of the church are aimed at putting people into a position where they can truly hear and receive the Gospel of Jesus Christ—they are like bait on a hook to draw people to Christ. Other programs are ones that teach God's Word or allow for distribution of God's Word around the world. The "business" of the church is the business of taking what is given and turning it into messages, activities, programs, and structures that bring glory to God and that produce fruit that lasts for eternity.

Our rewards for giving come back to us in practical ways on this earth. At the same time, they produce eternal fruit and eternal reward!

9. Our Giving Is to Be Cheerful and Consistent

The Bible declares, *"God loveth a cheerful giver"* (2 Corinthians 9:7). A cheerful giver is a person who gives spontaneously from the heart with joy—he doesn't give *"grudgingly"* or *"of necessity."* In other words, he doesn't give because he feels guilt-tripped into giving and hounded into giving. Rather, he gives because he delights in giving!

Surely if a person catches a glimpse of all the rewards and eternal benefits associated with giving...he will *want* to give—generously, frequently, and consistently. He'll look for ways in which to give, not ways to avoid being asked for a gift!

God also tells us in His Word that we must be consistent and diligent in our giving. We must persevere in giving, not growing weary in it but enduring in our commitment to obey. The Bible tells us, *"Let us not be weary in well doing: for in due season we shall reap, if we faint not"* (Galatians 6:9).

10. Your Giving Will Be More Than Matched by God

God's Word is clear. It declares, *"Be not deceived; God is not mocked: for whatsoever a man soweth, that shall he also reap"* (Galatians 6:7).

What you give is what you get back. Every farmer knows that principle—plant kernels of corn, get corn plants...plant beans, get beans. If you sow seeds of righteousness, which the Bible describes as sowing to the Spirit, you will reap the rewards associated with righteousness, which is being in right standing with God. Those rewards include financial blessing. (See Galatians 6:8.)

Like breeds like. But...with God there's a huge difference in one respect: God doesn't give back only what you give to Him. He gives back more. As I have already stated, the promises of God related to giving always point toward increase and multiplication. His giving back to us is measured in terms of thirty-fold, sixty-fold, and hundred-fold blessings. His desire is to *increase* His people and to *increase* their influence on this world, and as a result, to *increase* the numbers of people who will give honor and glory to His name, not only on this earth but throughout eternity.

MAKE A COMMITMENT:

"I will make no more excuses—I *will* tithe
regularly. I *will* believe God to be faithful
to His Word and to pour out
His blessing on my life."

Visit online at www.dennisleonardministries.com.

7

GOD'S CONTRACT WITH YOU

Have you ever thought about the fact that you have a contract with God? The party of the first part—that's *you*—and the party of the second part—that's God—agree to fulfill the stipulations outlined in the contract. If the first party doesn't fulfill their part of the bargain, the second party is under no obligation to fulfill His.

God's contract with you regarding your increase, your blessing, your multiplication, is really that simple.

The covenant agreement that God has with you calls for you to put Him first in your life and to bring your tithes into the storehouse, the local church. That's your part. His part is to bless every area of your life and to pour you out a blessing that is so great you won't have room to contain it.

If you don't tithe, God is under no "agreement" to bless you. Your failing to tithe blocks the fullness of His blessings from entering your life.

What's Shared...And What's Not Shared

The Bible tells us there are three things God doesn't share with man.

55

- He doesn't share His glory. The Bible gives us this word of the Lord: *"I am the LORD: that is my name: and my glory will I not give to another, neither my praise to graven images"* (Isaiah 42:8).

- He doesn't share His vengeance. We are commanded *not* to judge or condemn others, or to execute vengeance upon them. *"Dearly beloved, avenge not yourselves, but rather give place unto wrath: for it is written, Vengeance is mine; I will repay, saith the Lord"* (Romans 12:19).

- He will not share His tithe. *"And all the tithe of the land, whether of the seed of the land, or of the fruit of the tree, is the LORD'S: it is holy unto the LORD"* (Leviticus 27:30).

It is up to us to ascribe all glory to God...to give God total freedom to deal with other people as *He* sees fit...and to give the tithe.

What does God share? He shares all of His eternal riches in Christ Jesus. He gives us everything we need for our protection, provision, and accomplishment of His plan and purpose for us on this earth. He shares His wisdom, His ability to love, His joy, and His character.

God has given so much to us—salvation, protection, provision, peace, joy, love, and blessings too numerous to count. If you focus on all that God has given to you, and then you start thanking and praising the Lord for all He has done, is doing, and promises to do, you won't find it difficult to obey, trust, or love Him.

The Vital Clauses in God's Contract

God's contract with us regarding our prosperity has some very specific clauses. Each of them is vitally important.

The "Stop Stealing" Clause. God's contract with us in Malachi 3 says that we *"rob God"* when we refuse to pay our tithes. To rob God means we are stealing from Him!

I often have wondered how long people think they can et away with stealing God's stuff. It's as if they think God doesn't really know if they are tithing or not. God, who created the heavens and earth and who knows all things, certainly knows how much you get in your paycheck each week!

God's Contract with You

Others think that God will cut them some slack in their disobedience. They say, "Well, I'll give three percent this week because we are scheduled to go on vacation and we haven't had a vacation in a long time and I think God understands that we need to get away. Anyway, I'll make it up when we get back." Who do they think they are to try to barter with God? And the truth is, they rarely "make it up" when they return. They find other reasons not to give the full tithe, including paying for their overspending while they were on vacation!

God's Word is non-negotiable. His commandments are absolute. And very directly, let me say, His commandments apply to *you*. All of them.

The "Prove Me" Clause. It's okay to put God to the test. He said to *"prove"* Him! If you have never tithed before, I recommend that you make a ninety-day commitment to tithing. Tithe ten percent of your total income for ninety days and see what God does in your life.

The "Bring It Now" Clause. Don't delay in tithing! So many people say they will start tithing when they get a raise...when they pay off the car...when the children are out of school. The day never comes! In the meantime their finances spiral downward, not upward. I recently heard about three people who said they were going to make a major gift to God's work "just as soon as they made one more deal"—or in the case of one person, "one more real estate sale." Those gifts were never made. In each instance, the person *lost* money on the next deal. *Today* is the day to start obeying God in your finances. Don't delay or make excuses for not obeying.

The choices you make about tithing bring you into blessing...or push you out of blessing.

The "Huge Blessing" Clause. God tells us that if we will bring the firstfruits of ten percent to Him, He will pour out a huge blessing on the other ninety percent. The blessing will be so huge we won't be able to contain it! I don't know about you, but I would rather have ninety percent of my income blessed by God than have a hundred percent of my income under a curse.

God's intention for us is always for good. He delights in pouring out huge blessings on us. Jeremiah 29:11 is a passage I encourage you to memorize and pray often into your life:

For I know the thoughts that I think toward you, saith the LORD, *thoughts of peace, and not of evil, to give you an expected end.*

God's Way Works!

"In 1993, at the age of thirty-one, while visiting my mother, I gave my life to the Lord. I wasn't sure what I was going to do, because I didn't know any other lifestyle than what I had been in—and it wasn't good. I told my mother, 'I have given my life to the Lord'—even though I did not really know what that meant—'so if anyone calls from my past, I don't want to talk.'

"I had always made money from hustling, so my first fear was, *How am I going to make a living?* I only had a high school education, no work history, and very low self-esteem. My thinking was, *No one is going to give me a job making very much money.* I just knew I would end up like Al Bundy on the show "Married with Children," a saved shoe salesman.

"I tried everything I knew to make an honest living, only to end up evicted from our apartment, homeless, and living in a motel with my wife and three of my children during Thanksgiving, Christmas, and New Year's. My wife and I—mainly my wife—sold costume jewelry to pay the daily fifty-dollar motel bill to keep a roof over our heads. All the while I was wondering, *Where is God? I thought He was going to bless us.*

"The Lord spoke to us and told us to move from Texas back to Denver, Colorado. That's when God began to move. I stopped trying to get God to bless my plans and I asked Him to tell me what His purpose was for my life.

"First He said, 'Find a church for all people.' I asked around and people kept telling me to go to Heritage Christian Center. I obeyed. Second He said, 'Go to the school of ministry' that was at Heritage Christian Center. I obeyed. Third He said, 'Read the entire Bible from cover to cover.' I obeyed. Fourth He said, 'Stay under authority'—meaning the church leadership. I am still obeying.

"In October 1997 I was working a job at the airport that paid only eight dollars an hour, all the while going to the School of Ministry full-time, serving in the church, and being faithful. I began to realize that finances were tied to obedience, sacrifice, and authority. ***(continued)***

58

God's Contract with You

God desires the best for you. He has a future mapped out for you that is great. Get into obedience and start experiencing it!

The "Ever-Expanding" Clause. God's purpose in our bringing the tithes to His storehouse is so the Gospel can go forth and more souls can be saved. His purpose is to grow His kingdom in an ever-expanding way.

God's Way Works!

"The money didn't come right away, but the favor of the Lord began to move upon my family. People began to give us things—washer, dryer, TV, stereo, furniture, and much more. I knew it had to be God because when I did things the world's way, no one gave me anything. More favor came, and I was appointed to positions I was not qualified for, all the while thinking, *When are they going to find out that I don't know what I'm doing?*

"One day I was asked to fly with Bishop Leonard as a personal assistant for his road trips. Soon after that I was offered a job at the church to be the department head over the disciples' ministry. I accepted the offer, even though I didn't even know what being a department head meant! Eventually I became a licensed minister and I am now an Associate Pastor of one of the greatest churches in America!

"I began traveling even more with Bishop Leonard. The only discouraging part was hearing him preach on how a Christian was supposed to possess the land, own property, and that a 'good man leaves an inheritance to his children, and his children's children.' It seemed as though I had heard it hundreds of times, but I was not yet living it.

"My wife and I made a decision to plant continual seed for the miracle we needed. It took us almost seven years to climb out of the debt we were in, but we continued to pay the creditors one by one and straighten out incorrect items.

"To make a long story short, we are debt free. We went from zero income and staying in my mother's basement in 1997 to earning sixty-eight thousand dollars in 2003. To top it all, we recently moved into our first home, our brand-new home, that cost $260,000. We paid nothing down, and they actually gave us money back when we closed to pay off some other remaining debts. We even had enough left over to buy curtains and other items. Now we are doing everything we can to help others be blessed financially and to own property." — Pastor Clarence

Your partnership with God means you are a partner in the business of winning people to Christ and growing the kingdom of God. Your money given to the church makes you a soul winner, a feeder of the poor, a giver to missionaries, and so on. The fruit of your giving is a heavenly treasure. (If your church isn't producing fruit for the God's kingdom, perhaps you need to find a church that is!)

Your part in the ever-expanding kingdom of God, of course, means that you have a blessing awaiting you in heaven, as well as one waiting for you to experience here on earth. You will never run out of blessing—not for all eternity—if you will obey God.

The "All Glory to God" Clause. Stop to think for a moment: To whom does the blessing ultimately point? It points back to God! It points to Jesus, the one whom the blessed person proclaims as Savior. The blessing on your life doesn't just build you up to the point where others will admire you and respect you...it puts you in a position to *be* a blessing to others, and as you are a blessing to others, they will admire you and respect you. The blessing on your life doesn't just cycle back to you, but it also brings glory to God, your heavenly Father!

The "Devourer Rebuked" Clause. When you give to God as an act of your trust and faith in Him, He rebukes every enemy from your life—poverty, sickness, discouragement, and more. Every person has something that is coming against him to destroy his peace, finances, marriage, relationship with his children, his career, his ministry, his dreams. The thing that is coming against you with a goal of destroying you, your marriage, or your family...defeating you...damaging your integrity...diminishing your reputation or effectiveness...or denting your material worth...is something from the enemy of your soul, the devil and his minions. Jesus said, *"The thief cometh not, but for to steal, and to kill, and to destroy"* (John 10:10). It is the work of the devil to hurt you in any way he can.

God's promise is to rebuke the devourer. To rebuke is to reprimand in such a sharp and strong way that the behavior is *stopped.* That what God says to the devil. He says, "Stop. No more. You can steal no more, kill no more, destroy no more. Cease and desist and do so right now!" God has the authority to speak to the devil in this way, and the devil—who is not an equal to God but far beneath God in authority and power—must obey.

The Bible tells us that when the thief is found out, he must repay what he has stolen seven-fold (Proverbs 6:31). You may have lost a lot in your life. Multiply it by seven! That's what the devil is going to have to give up. That's what God has ordained for you, and it's time you put yourself into position to receive it.

As you give your tithes and offerings, pray to your heavenly Father, "Lord, I'm trusting *You* to rebuke the devil off my life. I'm trusting You to restore seven-fold what the devil has stolen from me."

The Blessing That Comes to Those Who Tithe

God's Word speaks of a very diverse blessing that comes upon those who obey His commandments and give their tithe. One of those blessings is a flow of God's presence and power in their lives.

As a pastor, I can assure you that those who tithe get more revelation out of church than those who don't. They receive more spiritual blessings, including healings. Those who tithe are those who seek to be obedient and, as such, they are usually obedient in all areas of their lives, not just in tithing. The result is there are no barriers between themselves and the wonder-working power of God or His awesome loving and eternal presence.

Those who tithe have insight into how they should respond to people around them. King Solomon, considered the wisest man who ever lived, prayed this:

> *Give therefore thy servant an understanding heart to judge thy people, that I may discern between good and bad: for who is able to judge this thy so great a people?* (1 Kings 3:9)

King Solomon wanted to be able to judge the character of other people. He knew God would have to give him this ability. And let me ask you, how many problems in your life could you have avoided if you had been able to judge more accurately the character or spiritual heart of another person who hurt you, rejected you, or caused you pain or loss?

Expanded Favor with People. God's Word doesn't stop with a rebuke of the devourer against your life. Malachi 3:12 says, *"And all nations shall call you blessed: for ye shall be a delightsome land, saith the LORD of hosts."* Because of the blessing that comes from tithing, other people will look at you and say, "The Lord has surely blessed you." The success and blessing you receive will be an encouragement to others.

When people call you "blessed," they are giving you a compliment. They recognize that you are in favor with the Lord. Generally speaking, people are quick to call others blessed because they have benefited in some way by being in associated with the blessed person.

Let me give you an example of this.

Think for a moment about a person who goes into an impoverished and disease-riddled community. The person doesn't just strut through that community with his fancy clothes and jewelry, or drive through that community in a fancy car. If the person did that, he probably wouldn't be called "blessed" by the folks who saw him. They might curse him or speak words rooted in jealousy.

No...this person we are thinking about goes into this community with humility and the love of Christ and begins to do what he can do to help the people who are poor and sick. He gives them the best news of all—the truth of the Gospel. He teaches them how to trust God with their lives, how to be forgiven of their sins through accepting Jesus as their Savior, and how to get into the flow of God's blessings. He gives them all the practical help he can, from teaching them about hygiene to giving them medicines he has purchased to teaching them how to develop skills that will enable them to work and earn money.

What are the people in that community likely to say when they see that man? They are going to shake his hand and say, "Bless you. Thank you." When the man walks away, they are going to say behind his back, "He's a great man. He's blessed by God, and he's a blessing to us!"

When God says that His people are going to be called "blessed" by all nations, He is saying that their reputation is going to be one of giving, of helping, of ministering. The people of the earth are going to look at who they are, what they believe, what they have, and what they do with what they have, and they are going to come to a conclusion, "These are blessed people!"

Tithers have favor wherever they go. The world doesn't always even fully know *why* they favor the person. There's just something about a person who trusts God fully and gives to God faithfully that is attractive, appealing, winsome.

Be Like Hezekiah!

One of the greatest examples of tithing and an abundance of "harvest" is found in 2 Chronicles 29–32. When Hezekiah came to the throne, he was only twenty-five years old. He reigned twenty-nine years and the Bible describes him as a man who *"did that which was right in the sight of the LORD"* (2 Chronicles 29:2).

From the very outset of his reign, Hezekiah opened the doors of the house of the Lord and repaired them. He ordered the Levites to sanctify themselves and the house of the Lord, and to put into place all things that pertained to worship as God had commanded it. Hezekiah then gathered together the rulers of the city of Jerusalem and they brought a sin offering that was intended to be for all Israel. This was done with great singing and worship, and from that day on, *"the service of the house of the LORD was set in order"* (2 Chronicles 29:35). Not only was the house of the Lord cleansed, but the Levites were appointed into their respective jobs to offer burnt and peace offerings, to *"minister, and to give thanks, and to praise in the gates of the tents of the LORD"* (2 Chronicles 31:2).

Next, Hezekiah invited the leaders throughout the land to come to Jerusalem to keep the Passover feast. In essence, the revival that had started in Jerusalem spread across the land as these leaders returned to their homes after the Passover. It was a time of tremendous healing, and that healing movement began with the king. The Bible tells us, *"Hezekiah prayed for them* [those who had erred and not cleansed themselves before eating the Passover], *saying, the good LORD pardon every one that prepareth his heart to seek God, the LORD God of his fathers...and the LORD hearkened to Hezekiah, and healed the people"* (2 Chronicles 30:18–20).

The third major thing that Hezekiah put into place was obedience when it came to tithing. Hezekiah didn't just command others to tithe. He *"appointed also the king's portion of his substance for the burnt offerings, to wit, for the morning and evening burnt offerings, and the burnt offerings for the sabbaths, and for the new moons, and for the set feasts, as it is written in the law of the LORD"* (2 Chronicles 31:3). The Bible tells us:

> *As soon as the commandment came abroad, the children of Israel brought in abundance the firstfruits of corn, wine, and oil, and honey, and of all the increase of the field; and the tithe of all things brought they in abundantly. And concerning the children of Israel and Judah, that dwelt in the cities of Judah, they also brought in the tithe of oxen and sheep, and the tithe of holy things which were consecrated unto the LORD their God, and laid them by heaps* (2 Chronicles 31:5–6).

What happened when this entire nation tithed? Great prosperity broke out in all corners of the land! The people were spared in a miraculous way the assault of Sennacherib, king of Assyria. They experienced a "golden age" of blessing!

In Hezekiah's personal life, he developed a pattern of putting God first. As a result, he reaped tremendous personal blessings as king. The Bible tells us that Hezekiah *"wrought that which was good and right and truth before the LORD his God. And in every work that he began in the service of the house of God, and in the law, and in the command-ments, to seek his God, he did it with all his heart, and prospered"* (2 Chronicles 31:20–21).

Hezekiah's prosperity wasn't limited to things spiritual or emotional. His blessing included great material wealth. God's Word also says,

> *Hezekiah had exceeding much riches and honour: and he made himself treasuries for silver, and for gold, and for pre-cious stones, and for spices, and for shields, and for all man- . ner of pleasant jewels; storehouses also for the increase of corn, and wine, and oil; and stalls for all manner of beasts, and cotes for flocks. Moreover he provided him cities, and*

God's Contract with You

possessions of flocks and herds in abundance: for God had given him substance very much (2 Chronicles 32:27–29).

Let me remind you of several truths we've covered already in this book:

- Put God first. Hezekiah did just that!

- Pray and study God's Word. Hezekiah did. He didn't have a Bible to read as we have the Bible to study. But he was a man who frequented the temple regularly, heeded God's Word, put into place all things in accordance with the law and commandments, and offered regular sacrifices and prayers.

- Obey the commandments. Not only did Hezekiah obey, but he also set the tone for obedience throughout the land.

- Put your faith in action with your giving of firstfruits. Hezekiah didn't just believe God in a private, quiet way. He proclaimed what he believed to every corner of his kingdom. He gave as an act of his faith. He obeyed God in the tithe and...

He prospered! Very few people in the recorded history of Israel prospered more than Hezekiah! His name is associated with goodness and his reputation was one of honor.

Start Praising God for His Contract with You!

Start praising God for all that He has for you as you begin to tithe and believe for God's outpouring of blessing in your life. Declare with joy that your own personal "year of Jubilee" is *this year*. Start anticipating God to set you free from the bondage of debt and financial crisis, and to turn the curses that you have struggled under into blessings so great you cannot contain them!

The year 1998 was declared a year of Jubilee in the nation of Israel. Jubilee comes every fifty years and Israel was fifty years old as a nation in 1998. In the Old Testament, the Jubilee year was the year when every slave was set free and all debts were canceled. Seven years of plenty followed a Jubilee year.

I have no doubt that I personally and the church I pastor are living in Jubilee years. God is getting His people ready for great things ahead! Here is what happened at Heritage Christian Center:

- In 1998, Heritage Christian Center paid off all its debts.

- In 1998, our lenders discovered that we had $500,000 in a sinking fund, which we didn't know anything about.

- In 1998, God paid off $16 million worth of debt!

I don't think it is at all accidental or coincidental that God allowed for Heritage Christian Center to be paid off in the year of Jubilee!

The year of Jubilee in the Bible always began with the blowing of the shofar, a type of trumpet made from the horn of an animal. Did you know that you have a trumpet in your mouth? It's time to proclaim your year of Jubilee by letting praise to God come forth from your lips! Praise Him, and keep praising Him, until you see the blessings come!

MAKE A COMMITMENT:
"I accept God's contract offer. I'm 'signing on' with praise in my heart and a commitment to giving!"

8

QUESTIONS AND ANSWERS ABOUT TITHING

People tend to have a strong opinion about giving to the church. Let me address a number of the statements, questions, and concerns I've heard through the years.

"Giving to charities is the same as giving to the church."

A significant number of people hold to the opinion that if they give to charitable organizations—secular or Christian in nature—they are giving their tithe to God. That simply is not what the Word of God says. The tithe is to be given to the *storehouse* of God, which is the local church. The place where you are routinely being spiritually fed is where your tithe is to go. God's Word says, *"Bring ye all the tithes into the storehouse, that there may be meat in mine house"* (Malachi 3:10). The purpose of your tithe is to fund the ministry of the Lord in *your* place of worship.

"All the preacher ever talks about is money."

I have overheard this statement a number of times—people rarely say this to my face as a preacher. I have two basic responses. First, I have never met a preacher who *only* talks about money. Perhaps the only sermons or statements these people are hearing and remembering are statements about giving because they aren't giving and the Holy Spirit is convicting them to give!

Second, one reason a preacher talks about money is because people aren't obeying God. A preacher desires for his people to be in obedience to God's commandments, to receive the fullness of God's blessings, and to see the work of the church go forward, not backward.

My question back to those who make this statement is this: "Are you willing to hear the voice of your pastor when he calls for the tithes and offerings?" The Bible says, *"Believe in the LORD your God, so shall ye be established; believe his prophets, so shall ye prosper"* (2 Chronicles 20:20). You must believe God's prophets in order to prosper. The opposite is equally true—if you don't believe them, you will not prosper in the totality of your life.

It is God who commanded the giving of tithes and offerings. The preacher will answer to God about how well he presents the commandments and whether he diligently and correctly preaches the Word. You will answer to God for how diligently and faithfully you keep the commandments.

"It doesn't really matter if I tithe regularly or give a full ten percent."

People always seem to be looking for shortcuts and then trying to justify them when it comes to keeping God's commandments. God calls the tithe "holy," and what God calls "holy" we should call "holy"!

The Lord spoke through the prophet Malachi, *"Will a man rob God? Yet ye have robbed me. But ye say, Wherein have we robbed thee? In tithes and offerings. Ye are cursed with a curse: for ye have robbed me, even this whole nation"* (Malachi 3:8–9).

Robbing God is a serious matter. In plain language, when you spend the tithe on your own desires, you are stealing from God and from His work on this earth.

68

Questions and Answers About Tithing

God gives us ninety percent with which we can do virtually anything we desire that is legal and moral. There's nothing wrong with buying a new car or a new suit with that ninety percent. There's nothing bad about getting your hair done or investing your money. The ninety percent is ours to do with as we desire.

"But I don't have enough to pay my bills and tithe, too," a person may say. The answer is, "Lower your bills." You may need to move to a different apartment. You may need to sell your expensive car and drive a cheaper one for a while. You may need to cut up your credit cards and quit spending more than you make. The bills aren't the problem. The way you have made choices to acquire those bills is the problem. Live within the ninety percent and give God the ten percent, and before long, God will have prospered you to the point the ninety percent will be increased.

"Do I really have to give *ten percent*?"

Some people teach that just "giving"—any amount, any percentage—is acceptable.

Numbers have meaning in the Hebrew language, just as words have meaning. The number seven, for example, has been associated with perfection or completion. The number six is associated with man. The number ten is associated with two very important concepts. It is associated with the fullness of the law—as in the Ten Commandments. The number ten is equally associated with the concept of "increase." The two concepts work together—in the fullness of obedience to the law, there's increase!

The ten percent that is the tithe is rooted in this wonderful truth: As you obey the Lord's commandments and trust in Him by giving your tithe, He will increase you.

"All this talk about God's blessings is just materialism in disguise."

Materialism seems to be a term that comes up fairly frequently when prosperity and blessing are emphasized. The truth is, every time you give to God with a forgiving, loving, and generous heart, you *break* the hold that materialism has on you. The cure for greed is to give. Martin Luther

69

taught that a man has three conversions—one in his head (to believe God's Word and the truth about Jesus as Savior), one in his heart (to trust God's faithfulness and receive God's mercy), and one in his wallet.

I can always tell when a person is in position to be blessed. That person starts putting the Lord first by obeying His commandments and giving in every way possible. He gives the best of his money to the church...the best of his time...the best of his talents and skills. God gave us His best in His Son, Jesus. Our response should be to desire to give Him our best.

Materialistic people hoard what the self perceives to be the "best." People with genuine generosity, love, and obedience give their best to God. The desire is to receive God's best in every dimension of life, including financial freedom.

It's important for you to ask, "Who's in control when it comes to my spending?" Do things seem to "call your name"? Do you become so obsessed with the idea of purchasing or owning a particular item that you can hardly think of anything else? Do you make your first thought in the morning and your last thought at night a thought about how you can get ahead, earn more money, improve your bank balance, make more lucrative stock purchases, acquire more possessions, or have tomorrow what you don't have today? If so, money is controlling you.

Choose to say "no" to the desires of your flesh. Instead, choose to exert control over your spending. Choose to give your tithe and offerings. Choose to obey God.

"The tithe isn't for today. It's only an Old Testament rule."

The tithe is a principle of God and the principles of God go from generation to generation. God taught Abraham to tithe hundreds of years before Moses wrote down the Law of God. The tithe is not related to a certain church, denomination, pastor, or cause. It's part of man's covenant relationship with Almighty God.

"I think it's good to give, but I don't think I should expect *anything* back."

Some people don't like the idea of expecting a return when they give of their tithe to the church. The Bible, however, says that this is a promise to us and the reason for our faith is so we might *expect* the promises of God to be realized or "come to pass" in our lives! Remind yourself of God's Word:

- *"Jesus said unto him, If thou wilt be perfect, go and sell that thou hast, and give to the poor, and **thou shalt have treasure in heaven**: and come and follow me"* (Matthew 19:21).

- [Jesus said,] *"Give, and **it shall be give unto you**; good measure, pressed down, and shaken together, and running over, shall men give into your bosom. For with the same measure that ye mete withal it shall be measured to you again"* (Luke 6:38).

"I'm too poor to give."

That is never truly the case. No matter how much you have in the way of material substance, you have *something* to give.

There's nothing good about poverty. It torments people. It causes people to worry. It steals a person's joy. And in some cases, it causes people to become so preoccupied with what they have that they become stingy.

God does not look at the dollar amount a person gives. He looks at the *percentage* that is given. He looks at the love and faith in a person's heart—the person's desire to obey His commands and trust Him with all of his life. Jesus made this very clear on the day He saw a widow giving an offering in the temple. She had given two mites, the smallest of Jewish coins. Jesus pointed out this woman to His disciples and said, *"Of a truth I say unto you, that this poor widow hath cast in more than they all: for all these have of their abundance cast in unto the offerings of God: but she of her penury hath cast in all the living that she had"* (Luke 21:3–4).

Jesus applauded her giving, her faith, her total dependency upon the Lord. He didn't at all evaluate the monetary amount of her gift. He saw it only in comparison to what she had available to give. He saw her heart.

When you tithe you are declaring your total dependence on the Lord and your independence from the world's economic system. It is a spiritual decision based on God's Word.

The tithe is actually a tool that seems to be of special help to those who are having a difficult time making it financially. It helps them lean on the Lord in a whole new way. It helps them declare their deliverance from financial bondage.

"I'll give when things improve."

I personally learned a long time ago that the foundation for all of God's blessings is to give. I seek to give in every situation, even the negative ones. It's usually when things get tough that people hold back. Don't do that. That's precisely the time to give.

Isaac, the son of Abraham, found himself living through a drought that produced a famine. The land became parched and resources ran low. Isaac was told specifically by God not to go down into Egypt, but to dwell in the land God would show him. Isaac obeyed.

The Bible tells us, *"Isaac sowed in that land, and received in the same year an hundredfold: and the LORD blessed him. And the man waxed great, and went forward, and grew until he became very great"* (Genesis 26:12–13).

From the world's standpoint, Isaac was foolish for remaining in a land plagued by famine, especially when sufficient pasture for the flocks and herds was located just a couple of weeks' journey away and food could be purchased in Egypt to sustain life with ease. From the world's standpoint, Isaac was foolish to sow good seed in a drought-stricken land. From the world's standpoint, tithing is going to seem foolish in good times, much less in bad times.

From *God's* perspective, however, sowing in a land of famine was precisely the wise thing to do. From God's perspective, tithing is always the wise thing to do, regardless of external circumstances, prevailing market trends, or the current economic forecast. Isaac received a hundred-fold increase on what he sowed! The truth is, God blesses obedience. Do what God commands and then watch God work on your behalf.

Blessings don't come when you have enough *money* to give. They start coming when you have enough *faith* to give. Stop making excuses for why you aren't tithing. Do you find yourself making the statements below?

- If I had a better job, I could give more.
- If my former spouse would just make his childcare payments on time, I could give.
- If I had more education, I could do more, and then I could give more.
- If my spouse would just get a job, we could afford to tithe.
- If I get this raise, I'll start tithing.

Excuses, excuses, excuses. None of them holds water with God.

People who start any sentence with "if" are trusting in circumstances to bring about change in their life. If you are trusting in circumstances, you aren't trusting in God!

MAKE A COMMITMENT:
"No more 'ifs' or 'whens' for me!
I'm tithing to God no matter what!"

Visit online at www.dennisleonardministries.com.

9

COME TO GRIPS WITH YOUR FINANCIAL SITUATION

Take stock of your financial situation. Are you pleased with the direction things are going? Do you enjoy an abundance of favor from God? Are blessings flowing to you in such a rapid and over-whelming way that you truly feel as if the windows of heaven have been opened and blessings have been poured out on you?

Or is everything going in a negative direction? The car won't start...the roof needs fixed...the kids are acting crazy...you keep having headaches...there just doesn't seem to be a good reason to get up in the morning?

Is your life headed in the direction of blessing or in the direction of a curse?

I have good news and bad news for you: It is *your* believing and *your* actions that determine the direction of your life and finances. Obedience to God and faith in God leads to blessing. Disobedience to God and a lack of faith in God leads away from blessing.

Some people seem to think that faith and planning are opposite. They aren't! Ask God to show you how to plan. The Bible promises us, *"I am the LORD thy God which teacheth thee how to profit, which leadeth thee by the way that thou shouldest go"* (Isaiah 48:17). Faith incorporates planning.

Practical Steps in Turning Things Around

Let me give you several practical steps to take.

1. Set financial goals for yourself and your family.

If you are married, you need to set goals in consultation with your spouse. Be of one mind and heart about what you intend to do with your money.

Sit down and write out your goals. Set some goals for the short-term, perhaps thirty, sixty, or ninety days. Set some goals for "this time next year" or "by the end of the year." Set some goals for the next three to five years.

"Is it biblical to set goals?" you may ask.

Yes, it is. The Bible tells us that all our plans and goals should be framed by these words, "as the Lord wills," which is another way of saying "as the Lord directs and allows." Sometimes we realize as we begin to pursue a plan that God has a different path for us to follow, or a higher goal to pursue. Listen to the Lord as you begin to set goals for yourself. Ask the Lord continually, "Is this what You desire for me? Is this the plan You want me to follow?"

Don't pull numbers and ideas out of thin air. Take a long hard look at where you are. You have to know where you're at before you truly can make a plan for *how* you are going to get where it is you desire to go.

There seems to be a very high percentage of people who don't truly know their financial situation. Sometimes a wife will choose not to know the family financial situation...sometimes one spouse purposefully keeps the other spouse in the dark about money matters...sometimes one or both spouses live in denial about the reality of their financial situation. They attempt to convince themselves that things are better than they truly are.

Come to Grips with Your Financial Situation

Get real with yourself. Get real with your spouse. Face the hard cold facts and numbers.

Set goals for yourself that are do-able...but that also challenge your faith.

One woman said to me, "I was making four hundred dollars a week. Someone told me that I should set a goal of making a thousand dollars a week. Well, Bishop, that may have been a good goal but it was a goal that just seemed too unbelievable to me. I couldn't wrap my faith around it. I set a goal of making four hundred and seventy-five dollars a week. That was a goal I could put my faith to...and it was a goal I reached in one year. Then I set a goal of five hundred and fifty dollars a week. I made that goal in two years. My next goal was seven hundred dollars a week. I made that goal last month. Now...maybe...I'm ready to set myself a goal of earning a thousand dollars a week in my business. My faith had to grow...just stretching it out and stretching it out. God has great things for me, I know that. I just have to get my faith and my heart and my mind believing what my Bible tells me is true."

Keep your goals handy so you can refer to them often. Celebrate with your spouse and family the accomplishing of a goal.

Here are some goals that are very much in line with both God's Word and good money-management principles:

- Get out of credit card debt

- Pay off all school and personal loans

- Pay off an automobile loan

- Save for the down payment on a home

- Put aside five hundred to a thousand dollars in a savings account as an emergency fund

- Open a retirement account and start putting money into it regularly

Write it Down. It is very important that you write out your financial goals and plans. Habakkuk 2:2–3 tells us, *"Write the vision, and make it plain upon tables, that he may run that readeth it. For the vision is* _yet for an appointed time, but at the end it shall speak, and not lie: though it tarry, wait for it; because it will surely come, it will not tarry."_

Writing down the vision God gives you for your finances will motivate you to achieve what you write down. You'll want to "run with it," as this passage from the Bible says. The vision you write down also will be a reminder to you in times when you feel discouraged—it will build up your faith and renew your ambition. The vision is for an _appointed_ time; in other words, God has already set the time for the vision to come to pass. When it does come to pass, you can look back at the vision you've written and say, "The vision was true!"

Be Patient. Hebrews 6:12 says, _"That ye be not slothful, but followers of them who through faith and patience inherit the promises."_ God's Word is true. When you do what the Word says to do, it is impossible for you _not_ to receive the promise. Sometimes we have to wait patiently for the promise—wait with faith and keep working!

2. Get realistic about what you _can't_ do and still reach your goal quickly.

Goals are mostly about what you can do, want to do, and believe you will do. There's one aspect to goals, however, that many people overlook and it's an important part of goal-setting. If you set a high goal for yourself, there are some things you no longer can do and still reach that goal in a timely way.

You can't be lazy. You'll have to give up some of your lazy habits.

You won't be able to do everything you want to do, whenever you want to do it. You'll have to learn to manage your time and make the most of every hour in a day.

You won't be able to waste money on things that are unimportant or unproductive. You'll have to make your money _count_ for something—make it work for you, instead of just you working for it.

You probably will have to make a decision to go on a cash-only basis. If you truly are going to get out of credit card debt, for example, you probably are going to need to cut up your credit cards, or as one person did, put them in water and freeze them for a while.

"But," you may argue, "I can still do some of these things and reach a goal—it may just take a little longer."

Come to Grips with Your Financial Situation

That's true...but not likely. Most people who don't stay focused on a goal abandon the goal because they don't see that they are making steady or sufficient progress toward reaching the goal. If a goal keeps getting pushed out farther and farther into the future, eventually there will be no motivation to reach that goal. It will fall into the category of a "Someday, I'll" wish.

3. Set some "action principles" for your life that are in line with spiritual principles.

An action principle is a principle that determines how you choose to act in a certain circumstance. Let me give you some good action principles that are in line with God's Word as they relate to your finances:

- I won't make a purchase of more than $20 without first discussing it with my spouse.

- I won't make a purchase of an item that isn't absolutely necessary unless I think about it for at least twenty-four hours.

- I will stop using credit cards and charge accounts. I will pay cash.

- I will put five percent of my income into a savings account until I have a thousand dollars saved as an emergency fund.

- I will look closely at the purchases of major items to see if there's a better time for me to make the purchase (or if a sale is coming up in the next few months).

Two of the most important action principles you can adopt are these:

- I will tithe regularly, beginning right now.

- I will make a budget and live within it.

A Vital Plan: Your Budget!

A vital part of your financial goal-setting and planning involves the making of a budget.

Make a Budget for the Month. Some people don't know how to make a monthly budget. Let me give you the basics:

1. Write down all of your income for the month, including your salary or wages, child support, tips, commissions, and so forth. If you don't know precisely how much you will have as income in a particular category (for example, tips), put down an estimate that is realistic based on the average of the last three month's worth of income in that category. Add up your income from all sources. This is your *total* monthly income.

2. List all of your fixed expenses for the month:

   • tithe

   • rent

   • car payment

   • utility bills

   • loan payments

   • insurance payments—such as health insurance, car insurance, and so forth. If an insurance payment comes up only every six months or every year, put down the amount that would apply to one month of the total bill. (For example, if your car insurance is $600 every six months, put down $100 in your monthly budget. Set aside that $100 and don't allow it to be spent for any other reason. You may even want to open a special savings account just for setting aside money to pay bills that are due only once or twice a year.)

   • credit-card or charge account payments (put down a number that is higher than the "minimum" on all cards that have an outstanding balance)

   • food—again, you may need to estimate

   Add up all of your fixed expenses. This is your total monthly expense figure.

3. Subtract your total monthly expenses from your total monthly income. This remainder amount is considered your "disposable net income."

Come to Grips with Your Financial Situation

4. Review your financial goals and determine how much of your disposable net income you can save toward future goals, such as a down payment on a house. I strongly encourage you to set aside *some* amount from your disposable income for savings.

5. Use the balance for "other expenses." Brainstorm with your spouse all the things that are likely to fall into that category. Include items such as haircuts, clothes, eating out, movies, pet food and veterinary bills, music lessons, dry cleaning, manicurist, make-up, and so forth.

Be aware that this "other expenses" category is where a lot of money likely is lost or unwisely spent every month. Talk about ways in which you can cut your expenses in this "other" category and put that money toward paying of your debts.

Spend According to Your Budget

It's one thing to make a budget. It's another to get into agreement with your spouse that you actually are going to spend your money according to that budget!

Be Creative in Finding Ways to Cut Expenses. It isn't enough for you to anticipate an increase in income to solve your financial problems. The vast majority of people need to cut expenses. We have been brainwashed to think that we *need* certain things in order to feel good about ourselves or to have status in society. What we *need* is the freedom to obey God and to do what He calls us to do quickly and generously. To have that kind of flexibility and freedom before the Lord requires that we become financially wise and financially free. Set yourself the goal of financial freedom. Pursue it with your whole heart.

Keep Track of Your Spending. I suggest you take "account" of your spending every week to make sure you are staying within the amounts you established in your budget. A budget helps you answer the question, "Where is my money going?"

Periodically Review the Numbers in Your Budget. Have your actual expenses changed in a category? For example, did you guess

81

too high or low on your food budget? Can you cut that number by taking lunches to work instead of eating out? Can you reduce your food budget by not stopping for coffee and a donut every morning on the way to work?

Set a New Budget Every Month

Don't plan a budget too far out into the future. Take each month as it comes. Some months may have special events in them. Various problems and emergencies may require extra spending in some categories in some months.

The Consumer Credit Counseling Services (CCCS) recommends the following guidelines as you figure a family budget:

- Tithe   10%
- Housing (mortgage or rent, taxes, insurance, repairs, improvements)   30–35%
- Utilities (gas, electricity, water, trash, sewer, cable, Internet, phone)   4–7%
- Food (groceries, pet food, dining out)   15–20%
- Auto/Transportation (car loan, gasoline, oil, repairs, insurance, parking, public transportation)   6–20%
- Medical (health insurance, dental bills, doctor bills, prescriptions)   2–8%
- Clothing (clothes, shoes, accessories, alterations, dry cleaning)   4%
- Investments/Savings   5–10%
- Personal and Miscellaneous (cosmetics, toiletries, hair, nails)   5–10%
- Credit Card Purchases   15%

Set a Goal to Live Debt-Free

Debt opens the door to all kinds of problems. Are you aware that money problems are the number one cause of marital difficulty?

Come to Grips with Your Financial Situation

Money problems can greatly damage a marriage. Many accusations and much arguing occur over when, where, why, and how much money is spent. Couples who fight over money often find they are feeling deep anger, resentment, and bitterness toward their spouse.

Debt is like a chain around your neck. Excessive debt enslaves people to the point that they can't obey God. For example, suppose God speaks to your heart to give a specific offering...but you can't do it because you have a bill due. Suppose God tells you He desires for you to go on a short-term missions trip...but you can't do it because you're behind on your credit card payments. Debt keeps you from the flexibility the Lord desires in your life so He can use you more mightily to spread the Gospel and grow the kingdom of God!

The more debt a person has, the harder it is for that person to operate in faith.

Nobody gets out of debt accidentally. It's easy to get into debt because you aren't paying attention to what you are spending. You *must* pay attention to what you are spending if you want to reverse the process.

It's not possible to experience financial freedom if you have debt. The two are incompatible. The Bible tells us clearly, *"The rich ruleth over the poor, and the borrower is servant to the lender"* (Proverbs 22:7). Debt is a slave driver.

The Bible also tells us, *"Owe no man any thing, but to love one another"* (Romans 13:8).

Set yourself to the *process* of getting out of *all* credit card, charge account, and personal loan debt. Work toward the day when you also can pay off your car and school loans, and then your home.

Debt can happen very quickly. Getting out of debt very often takes time. Trust God to pull you all the way through your debt to financial freedom. Commit yourself to doing what is necessary to do your part in controlling your spending and curbing your appetite for "things" that have no eternal value. Be a good steward of what God gives you.

Get Smart about Money

Some families have been ignorant about money for generations! Some people fail at managing money because they've never been taught how to manage it wisely. Now's the time to turn all that ignorance into wisdom. Now is the time to manage money well. Even if you've never been taught by your parents how to spend, save, and invest wisely...now's the time to learn!

"But how?" you may ask, "Where can I learn to manage money wisely?"

Here are five ways to get started.

- Look for a short course or a study program to learn how to manage money. Start with the basics. A course at your local community college may be a start. Perhaps your church offers a course in basic money management.

- Consider going to a seminar that is about investing. I'm not talking about going to a seminar that presents a get-rich scheme. I'm talking about an *informational* seminar that offers basics.

- Get around people who are prospering financially and talk to them about money matters. Be humble. Learn from them. Most people who are successful are willing to tell you what they know.

- Read about money. There are dozens of books about basic money management and investing. There are magazines devoted to money management.

- Above all, immerse yourself in the Word of God and become knowledgeable what the Bible says with regard to money and material substance. Gain all the Bible wisdom you can gain—make it the foundation for any other information you acquire.

MAKE A COMMITMENT:
"I will rule over my wealth rather than have debt rule over me."

10

TAKE CONTROL

S top looking for get-rich schemes.
Stop looking for an easy way out.

Quit blaming your race, age, gender, or culture as an "excuse" for why you can't get a job, keep a job, or be promoted.

The truth is, these are things you can't control. God requires you to take control of those things you *can* control and that He has given you the authority to control.

The vast majority of people today want to live "the good life"—but the vast majority also wants to have that good life be an "easy life." They don't want to have to work for the good life, sacrifice for it, or limit their own behavior in order to have it. The old saying "anything worth having is worth working for" is true! The best things in life take some effort. That's true for education, achievement, a successful career. It is also true for spiritual growth and maturity.

It's up to you—and nobody but you—to take control over matters related to your finances.

The good news is that God will empower you to do it if you will trust Him for wisdom and courage.

Control Your Spending

One of the most important decisions you can make in your life is to decide that you are going to control your spending and your finances, rather than have debt control you.

You know that debt is in control of you if you...

• Struggle to keep from being overdrawn in your checking account

• Routinely are late, or are even occasionally late, in making payments for your rent or mortgage, your utility bills, or your automobile

• Routinely are "maxed out" on all your credit card spending limits

• Are never able or are rarely able to pay more than the "minimum payment due" on a credit card account or charge account

• Routinely are late in making credit card or charge account payments, or if you routinely or occasionally "skip" making a payment

• Have more credit card or charge account debt this year than you had this time last year

• Have been denied the privilege of purchasing an item over time because you have a poor credit rating

There are only two ways to get out of debt. Make more money or cut back on spending. You can't always ensure that you'll make more money. You may, however, be able to sell some things you have but don't use regularly, to get some cash to pay your bills. It may be time for you to clean out your attic or garage or storage shed. See what you have that can be sold to pay your bills.

The prime way of getting out of debt is to cut back on spending. You may need to trade in your car on one that has a much lower payment. You may need to move to a place with a mortgage you can handle.

You definitely need to get out of credit card debt. Credit cards charge tremendously high interest rates. If you don't pay off your credit cards in full every month, you have excessive debt.

Take Control

Can You Say "No"? Do you have trouble saying "no" to something you want? If so, you are not alone. Many people have trouble saying "no" to an item that has great appeal to them. Saying "no," however, is an attribute of being a mature, responsible adult. It's also a hallmark of those who are disciplined. I'm not at all saying that you have to say "no" to all pleasure, luxuries, or fun in your life. You do need to say "no" to these things:

- Say "no" to sin.

- Say "no" to greed.

- Say "no" to debt.

The inability to say "no" to purchases is very often a sign of low self-esteem. People with low self-esteem often think that they need to have certain items so that others will value them or think well of them. They believe they are purchasing status, value, approval, or love—they don't see themselves as being worthy of the affection or association of important people unless they have certain things, such as a designer label on their clothing, expensive shoes, a popular wristwatch, a luxury automobile, and so forth.

If you have trouble saying "no" to purchases, ask yourself, "Am I trying to buy love? Am I trying to gain approval?"

Those who feel they must have the approval of other people sometimes don't understand that the "approval ratings" given by others fluctuate widely. Nobody likes everybody else all the time. Most people don't give unconditional love, at least not all the time.

Only God is capable of infinite and eternal unconditional love. Choose to receive the overflowing abundance of God's love into your life. He doesn't care in the least about the label on your clothes or the make and model of your automobile. He cares about the *real* you—the talents and skills and dreams and desires He has placed in your heart. He cares about you fulfilling your purpose on this earth. He cares about your love for Him and your obedience to His commandments. He cares about your acceptance of Jesus Christ as your Savior. He cares about your overcoming sin and greed and debt. He wants you to live in freedom and fullness—not shackled by purchases that are "in" one season and "out" the next, not bound up by debt for items that you've long since worn out or grown tired of. Choose to care about the things God cares about. Ask the Lord to adjust your self-esteem so that you can see how dearly you are loved and valued by Him!

Ultimately, God loves you, loves you, loves you solely because He created you. He values you because you are His handiwork.

Help for Controlling Your Spending

There are three tried-and-true practices that can help you control your spending habits:

1. Pay cash.

You are less likely to overspend when you use cash. Paying cash for items also allows you to have an "emergency" backup system in your credit cards. A credit card, however, can be a backup system only if you aren't already maxed-out on your spending limit!

When you pay cash, you are much less likely to engage in impulse shopping. It's tougher to hand over a twenty-dollar bill than it is to hand over a plastic charge card.

2. Consider a purchase in terms of how much it will *really* cost.

If you make a purchase using a credit card, and you don't pay off the full amount of that purchase in the month you made the purchase, you actually are taking out a "loan" to make the purchase. You will be paying interest on that loan until you have finished paying for the item. Before you charge an item, ask yourself, "Is it worth taking out a loan to buy this? How long will it take me to pay this off, and at what interest rate?" If you don't have a good answer to these questions, delay your purchase until you can pay cash for the item.

I recently heard about a young man who had just gotten out of charge account debt. For several years, he had a large balance at a local department store. He admitted that he had been paying on clothes for months after he had worn them out! He said, "One day I realized that because of all the interest I was paying and the amount of time I was taking to pay off my charge account, I had paid more than $60 for a shirt that I had originally purchased for a price of $28.

I thought the shirt was a good deal at $28. Paying $60 was outrageous! That's when I decided that it was cash only for me."

3. Don't wait to establish good credit.

Don't think that you can slide along with a bad credit rating and then suddenly "clean up" your credit when you decide to make a major purchase, such as a car or home. You need to start reviewing your credit history now. Creditors generally look at a twenty-four month history to evaluate a person's credit status. If you have had poor credit in the past, start cleaning up your credit. Make on-time payments and pay off your credit accounts.

Maintain Good Credit

As part of figuring out where you are financially, get a copy of your credit report. Once a year you can obtain a *free* copy of your credit report from each of the three main credit reporting agencies: Experian, Transunion, and Equifax. You can either write to them to request a copy or use the Internet to get your report. After you see what is on your report, you can start the process of taking care of late or unpaid accounts. Also make sure that any mistakes are cleared up. Some times there are mistakes on a credit report that can be removed.

If you need help in this area, contact your local non-profit credit counseling agency. These agencies are available to help you repair your credit by setting up a special payment plan for each of your creditors. The agencies also can help you negotiate your balances and the interest rate you may be paying.

A word of caution: Don't confuse these agencies with those that work for profit. For-profit credit agencies are not always reputable and they do not always help. The best resource to get your credit cleaned up is a non-profit consumer counseling agency. Most of them charge minimal fees, if they charge anything at all.

Change Your Purchasing Habits

Let me give you seven very practical do's and don'ts about your purchasing:

1. *Don't* make purchases based on what you think you "deserve." What you "deserve" can put you in bondage for the rest of your life. Make decisions based on what you can afford.

2. *Don't* buy into the lie that a "product" will make you sexier or more appealing to the opposite sex. Ultimately, people of the opposite sex respond to kindness, a heart that is caring, and an attitude of genuine interest.

3. *Don't* think carrying a big wad of cash makes you more important. It may make you slightly more vulnerable to assault and robbery, but it doesn't make you more important. (As for making you more vulnerable, if you aren't flashing that wad of cash around, who will know you have it? Thieves steal empty purses and wallets as often as they steal full ones, so the amount of money doesn't influence whether you'll be robbed. The way you handle your money and your *self* is a big factor.)

4. *Don't* assume that you will get a raise to pay off your debts. If you have that attitude, if you do get a raise, you are likely to plunge yourself into even deeper debt.

5. *Don't* pay retail for anything! Look for sales. Look for bargains. Shop secondhand stores and garage sales and outlet stores. Don't just look for "good deals"...look for the best deal on something you truly need.

6. *Don't* think that something is a "perfect purchase" just because it's on sale. Ask yourself, "Do I really need this? Can I afford this?" Some items shouldn't be purchased even if they are a fabulous deal! Some people shop sales and spend a tremendous amount of money on things they don't truly need and in some cases don't even like all that much simply because it was a bargain "too good to pass up." Any bargain is too expensive if you don't truly need the item!

7. *Do* buy only what honors God. Let me meddle in your life for a second. Your priorities are out of order if you struggle to pay your bills but still spend money on cigarettes and alcohol.

Also...*don't* buy into the lie that you "deserve to be making more money" and, therefore, you don't need to work as hard for the salary you are being paid. Work hard! Deserve to be promoted when the job opens up.

Take Control of Your Work Habits

Proverbs 10:4 tells us, *"He becometh poor that dealeth with a slack hand: but the hand of the diligent maketh rich."*

You may need to overcome some of your lazy attitudes and start working *hard*. God tells us the wealth of the wicked is stored up for the righteous—but He also tells us that a righteous man works to feed his family! (See Proverbs 13:22.) The apostle Paul advised the Christians in Thessalonica, *"Do your own business"* and *"work with your own hands"* (1 Thessalonians 4:11).

"But I can't get a job," you may be saying.

Then start your own business! Get yourself a bucket and a mop and go to work. Start in your basement—create something, make something, bake something....but most of all *do* something. Trust God to bless the work of your hands. A person who isn't doing anything is a person who has no reason to expect God to bless anything.

You need to rebuke your own laziness. Make up your mind to work hard and trust God.

Many people want a preacher to lay hands on them to cure all their problems. Living a life of wholeness and blessing isn't that simple. We are called to live out the plans and purposes of God. We are called to be willing and obedient. If you are asking God to heal you, pray for healing and then take steps to do what you can to eat right, live right, and take care of yourself!

If you want greater financial blessing, pray and trust God to meet your needs and then take steps to do what you know to do! Start giving, be diligent, take charge of your spending...financial freedom doesn't come by mysterious means. It comes by faith coupled with *action*.

Some of that action is plain old hard work.

Some of that action is putting into place wise financial plans.

Some of that action may be cutting up all your credit cards and going to a cash-only basis in your purchasing.

Some of that action may be opening a savings account or an investment account.

Some of that action *must* be giving to God what is rightfully God's.

Take Control of Your Giving

God isn't going to make you tithe. He isn't going to cut your spending. He isn't going to sit down at your kitchen table with you and make a budget for you. That would be nice, but it won't happen. The truth is, God has equipped you to do those things already. He expects you to do them because you have the ability to do them.

If you aren't controlling your spending...why not?

If you're blaming somebody else for your lack of financial wisdom...there's nobody to blame but the person who stares back at you from your own mirror!

People are in a financial mess because they've made that mess. Don't blame the devil. Don't blame another person. Don't blame the government or your former place of employment. Take charge of your financial life! Choose to conduct your finances according to God's plan.

MAKE A COMMITMENT:

"I will take control of my spending...my purchasing... my work habits...and my giving habits!"

Visit online at www.dennisleonardministries.com.

11

PUT AWAY ALL IDOLS

Your spending habits are a good indication of whether you have an idol in your life.

Do you spend a hundred dollars on clothes or shoes, and then put a five-dollar bill in the offering plate? If so, you're turning clothes and shoes into idols.

Do you go into debt for your beautiful new "dream car" and then decide that you don't have any money left to pay your tithe? If so, that car is an idol.

If your mortgage payment is so high you don't think you can pay your tithes and still live...you have placed a worldly possession higher than your obedience to God. That's idolatry.

For many people, money is an idol. A savings account, a bank balance, a stocks-and-bonds portfolio, or real estate holdings can be an idol in your life.

"Does God want me to give up all these things and be poor?" you may ask.

No! God wants you to prosper in all things. But above all, God doesn't want you to worship anything but Himself. He doesn't want you to worship the things He blessed you with!

Some people seem to think God wants them to be poor all their lives. Some people think money is evil. Neither is true! Money is only evil if you idolize it. The Bible says that *"the love of money is the root of all evil"* (1 Timothy 6:10). It isn't money that's evil—it's the *love* of money that makes money an idol. That same verse, 2 Timothy 6:10, goes on to say, *"Which while some coveted after, they have erred from the faith, and pierced themselves through with many sorrows."* Those who are always thinking about money and the things they can buy will *pursue* those things instead of pursuing God. The result will be pain and sorrow.

Idols Are More Than What You Think They Are

Let me remind you of the first two of the Ten Commandments:

Thou shalt have no other gods before me. Thou shalt not make unto thee any graven image, or any likeness of any thing that is in heaven above, or that is in the earth beneath, or that is in the water under the earth: thou shalt not bow down thyself to them, nor serve them (Exodus 20:3–5).

When you serve other gods, you open the door for the enemy to bring destruction to your life.

Now you may think that *"other gods"* is a reference to wooden or stone idols. However, it relates to a whole lot more than that. *Anything* you put before God in your life is an idol. An idol can be your spouse, your career, or time you spend watching television programs. An idol can be anything that you "pursue" more than you pursue your relationship with the Lord. It can be anything to which you look for your identity other than the Lord.

In the Old Testament, we see repeatedly that the children of Israel fell under a curse every time they fell away from serving God. It seems that one day they were serving God and prospering, and the next day they were doing their own thing or dabbling in worship to a false god. Immediately, they began falling into very difficult times.

They seemed continually to be sidetracked with things other than their obedience to and love for God.

God makes it clear—if you aren't serving Him *first*, then you really aren't serving Him.

So many Christians fall into a pattern that is very much like that of the Israelites. They trust God to direct them, and then the next day trust the horoscope in the local newspaper for direction. They go to church on Sunday, but then on Monday consult the call-in psychic. They say they love the Lord, but they don't spend time with the Lord. Rather, they spend time with everything and everyone other than the Lord!

Examine your own life. What's the "temperature" of your love for the Lord? Are you becoming cold spiritually?

There are people I know who need to pray and fast and turn the television set off for a month and spend some time with God. They need to get into His Word and get their minds and hearts back on track with what is true and what is required by God.

The good news is that God will move mountains for those who will get the idolatry out of their lives and put Him first. Every time the Israelites removed all other gods from their lives, the Lord began to bless them. The same is true for us today.

If the Lord called you to spend a day alone with Him, what would you do? Would you tell Him that you'd do that, except for the hour or two of your favorite soap operas? Would you tell Him you couldn't do that because of your job? Would you tell Him you couldn't spend that much time because you were right in the middle of a relationship that might not work out, "but I'll catch You later, Lord"?

Generational Curses and Blessings

I have mentioned in previous chapters the role of generational curses on our finances. Generational curses are those curses that go down from generation to generation—the same problems or tendencies to sin keep popping up again and again. The Lord speaks of this generational aspect of a curse as part of the Ten Commandments. The Bible says between the second and third commandments:

95

I the LORD thy God am a jealous God, visiting the iniquity of the fathers upon the children unto the third and fourth generation of them that hate me; and shewing mercy unto thousands of them that love me, and keep my commandments (Exodus 20:5–6).

Generational curses *can* be turned into generational blessings! The turnaround comes with *obedience*.

Yes, life can be hard. When life hits you with a tragedy, you may not care in that moment if you are walking under a blessing or a curse. You may feel hopeless. The sin in your heart may have put down such deep roots that you don't really care if you lose everything you have. In the end, however, a life under the curse is a life that is on a downward spiral to death. That pattern needs to be broken. If it isn't, you are in danger of passing on that downward spiral to your children. Choose instead to care about your life and to break every curse that is shackling you in the name of Jesus. Choose to obey God and trust God!

One of Satan's main targets seems to be marriage. If a marriage breaks up, the breakup destroys not only the husband and the wife, but also the children and many other relatives and friends. The breakup of a marriage has a strong ripple effect. It can influence people who are in the couple's church, who know them in the community, who live near them in the neighborhood. The breakup of a marriage is like a slam dunk for the devil. Satan knows there is blessing associated with marriage. When two people come together in a good marriage union, they multiply the power of God in their lives wherever they go. Deuteronomy 32:30 tells us that one may chase a thousand, but two can put ten thousand to flight! Marriage is a blessing to each spouse, to their children, and to their relatives, neighbors, friends, and so on. Those who walk under the blessing can experience great joy, peace, and happiness. They can find fulfillment in serving God together. And the blessing a couple experiences in marriage can impact future generations.

In my family, my father has always served God. He was not a perfect man, but he taught me to put God first and to tithe and give offerings. I remember him trusting God in his own business. He and my mother would write a check together as their tithe and offering. They believed God for the best in their business. The blessing they experienced in their lives was passed along to me. Even when I wasn't serving God and was questioning whether God even existed, I was still blessed because of the blessing that was on my father and passed down to me. Today, I pass that same blessing on to my sons. They have not done everything right just as I have not done everything right—but we walk under the blessing.

If your family heritage is one of blessing, rejoice in that fact and make a determination in your heart that you will continue that blessing to future generations.

If your family heritage has been one of walking under a curse, make a decision today that you and your family will be the ones who break that curse. Come into agreement: "We've been under the curse long enough. We proclaim that the curse is broken in the name of Jesus." Set yourselves to seeking God as the first priority in your lives and to obeying His commandments and statutes. As a family, become strong and united in doing what the Bible tells you to do. Choose to leave a holy legacy for the next generation!

Give Up the Idols!

I don't know the idols in your life. I don't know what you are "serving" more than you are serving God. I don't know what you are spending your tithe money on instead of giving it to God's storehouse. But I do know this—God has called you to give up that idol and to obey Him. He promises you a tremendous blessing if you'll do it. Read what His Word says:

Ye shall make you no idols nor graven image, neither rear you up a standing image, neither shall ye set up any image of stone in your land, to bow down unto it; for I am the LORD your God. Ye shall keep my sabbaths, and reverence my sanctuary: I am the LORD. If ye walk in my statutes, and keep my commandments, and do them; then I will give you rain in due season, and the land shall yield her increase, and the trees of the field shall yield their fruit. And your threshing shall reach unto the vintage, and the vintage shall reach unto the sowing time: and ye shall eat your bread to the full, and dwell in your land safely. And I will give peace in the land, and ye shall lie down, and none shall make you afraid: and I will rid evil beasts out of the land, neither shall the sword go through your land. And ye shall chase your enemies, and they shall fall before you by the sword. And five of you shall chase an hundred, and an hundred of you shall put ten thousand to flight: and your enemies shall fall before you by the sword. For I will have respect unto you, and make you fruitful, and multiply you, and establish my covenant with you. And ye shall eat old store, and bring forth the old because of the new. And I will set my tabernacle among you: and my soul shall not abhor you. And I will walk among you, and will be your God, and ye shall be my people (Leviticus 26:1–12).

God's promise to us is a promise of total provision, total fulfillment of goodness, total safety and security, and a life that is fruitful and marked by multiplication. He says we will be able to eat fully from what we have acquired because new acquisitions are on the way. He will *"walk"* among us, reveal Himself to us, and have spiritual fellowship with us.

What a blessed life! What more could any person possibly want?

Choosing to walk under the blessing of God is not a one-time decision. It's a choice you must make every day. You continually will be bombarded by temptations of the devil to open your life to sin or to serve the flesh. You must choose to obey God every time a temptation comes your way. Remind yourself continually that the choice you make determines blessing or curse.

Kick out any plan that doesn't line up with the Bible.

Walk away from any relationship, or any potential relationship, with an ungodly person.

Boot out any idol that causes you to put God and His commandments into a secondary position.

MAKE A COMMITMENT:
"I will have no idols in my life."

12

FOLLOW GOD'S CALL

G od calls us to a life of blessing.
God also calls us to a life of purity.

The two go together.

God's Word tells us, *"Let us lay aside every weight, and the sin which doth so easily beset us, and let us run with patience the race that is set before us"* (Hebrews 12:1). God says that if we truly are to walk in blessing, we must lay aside sin. Sin does nothing for us except trip us up, pull us down, and do us in!

You may be asking, "Are you telling me I have to live a perfect life?"

No. That's not possible. None of us can ever live a perfect life. Jesus lived the only perfect life on this earth. But...we each can do all that we know to do in keeping God's commandments and walking according to the principles of His Word.

Our perfection is the work of the Holy Spirit in us. He is the one who began and who will finish the work of conforming us totally into the character likeness of Christ Jesus.

Our work is to obey God, trust God, and be faithful to God to the best of our ability.

We all make mistakes and errors. Some mistakes we wouldn't make if we knew we were making a mistake. But some of the errors we make are willful ones. Either way, God's Word tells us that if we will immediately own up to our sin and ask for His forgiveness, He'll forgive us. His promise to us is this: *"If we confess our sins, he is faithful and just to forgive us our sins, and to cleanse us from all unrighteousness"* (1 John 1:9).

What God hates is a willful choice to continue in a *lifestyle of sin.* It is when we choose *not* to confess our sins or repent of them...when we choose repeatedly to engage in something we know is wrong...when we choose wrong over right as our automatic and routine choice...we're into a lifestyle of sinning. If you are living in a sinful relationship, consistently going where you shouldn't go, consistently doing what you shouldn't do, or habitually expressing an attitude that is the opposite of a godly nature, you are engaging in a lifestyle of sin. You need to make a decision. You need to face up to the fact that your sin is going to produce death, destruction, loss, and degradation in you. You need to seek God, confess your sin, start putting God first, and start obeying God's commandments.

In my experience as a pastor, I have met people from all walks of life and all kinds of backgrounds. Many times a lack of knowledge plays a huge part in their allowing sin in their lives. Let me share with you a few things that you may not know.

- Living a lifestyle of sin will bring destruction to your life. Drugs, alcohol, and sex outside of marriage are three examples of things that bring about destruction.

  Give up you lover.

  Put down the crack pipe.

  Quit cheating on your spouse.

  Quit cheating on your taxes.

- False idols—such as a statue of Buddha—should not be in your house. The wearing of occult jewelry or zodiac jewelry can put you into disobedience before God.

Follow God's Call

- Following a new age guru is a form of "following after" a false god and a false religion.

- Ouija boards, fortunetellers, tarot cards, and horoscopes should be cast out of your life.

- Jealousy, envy, bitterness, and an unclean heart—they gotta go!

- Stealing the tithe and spending it on your own self is a sure invitation to failure.

Reject any opportunity to engage in the sins of the flesh.

The Bible gives us a list of some of the *"works of the flesh."* They include *"adultery, fornication,* [moral] *uncleanness, lasciviousness* [lewdness], *idolatry, witchcraft* [sorcery], *hatred, variance* [contentious arguing], *emulations* [jealousies], *wrath, strife* [dissensions], *seditions* [selfish ambitions], *heresies, envyings, murders, drunkenness, revellings, and such like"* (Galatians 5:19–21).

A person once asked me what that final phrase *"and such like"* included. It includes anything that you intuitively suspect *might* be opposed to love, joy, peace, long-suffering (patience), gentleness, goodness, faith, meekness, temperance (self-control). If something isn't in line with these character qualities we know as the *"fruit of the Spirit"*—or if something doesn't produce these qualities in your life...run from it! It isn't of God and doesn't deserve even a glance from you.

Get serious about your walk with God. Don't experiment with...dabble in...explore...participate in...or even think about participating in things that you know are opposed to God's highest and best plan for you and your family.

Anything that comes before God is a danger to your destiny! If you have been involved in any of these things, confess your sin to God today, seek His forgiveness, and then change your ways! Reverse the curse, starting *now*.

If you have a question about anything you are doing, ask the Lord about it in prayer and look it up in His Word. If you are questioning whether something is right or wrong, in all likelihood it is wrong.

Are You Willing to Take Up Your Cross?

Jesus commanded His followers, *"If any man will come after me, let him deny himself, and take up his cross daily, and follow me"* (Luke 9:23). Jesus was not telling His disciples that they needed to take up literal wooden crosses and carry them around every day. He was telling His disciples that a life of following Him closely would mean sacrifice and self-denial. What did Jesus mean?

Sacrifice is honoring God with one's substance—money, possessions, and material wealth. Sacrifice means giving, according to God's commandments. Little token gifts aren't sacrificial gifts. Sacrificial gifts are ones that come from the heart and that are in full obedience to what God's Word requires.

Most people I know consider the tithe to be a sacrifice. It's not easy to give ten percent of what comes into your hands on payday. But when that gift to God's storehouse—the local church—is wrapped up in your love for God and given in obedience to what God has ordained, you are in right standing with God for your blessing.

What about self-denial? Self-denial is saying, "I will say 'no' to the temptations to worship myself or any other thing. I will say 'no' to greed and the temptation to 'rob' God. I will say 'no' to any lust of the flesh or lust of the eyes when it comes to the purchases I make and the places I make those purchases."

The Bible tells us plainly that we are to *"love not the world, neither the things that are in the world. If any man love the world, the love of the Father is not in him"* (1 John 2:15). Self-denial is saying "no" to the things of this world that pull us away from God and that seek to take first place or become a top priority in our life.

The Bible spells out what draws us away from God. *"For all that is in the world, the lust of the flesh, and the lust of the eyes, and the pride of life, is not of the Father, but is of the world. And the world passeth away, and the lust thereof: but he that doeth the will of God abideth for ever"* (1 John 2:16–17).

Lusts of the Flesh. The lusts of the flesh are those things that are experienced by the five senses—things that seem to satisfy for the moment but that need to be repeated again and again because they never *truly* satisfy. The lusts of the flesh are sexual, but these lusts also refer to food and beverages, chemical substances, and other things that produce momentary sensual "highs" for a person—these are lusts of the *flesh* that produce *physical* addiction.

Self-denial means saying "no" to these things. And saying "no" means we don't spend our money on these things...not just God's part of our income but *none* of our income should be spent on things that lead to addiction or that fuel a lust of the flesh.

Are sex and food bad? Not at all! But sex and food need to be part of our lives according to God's commandments! Sex belongs in marriage. Period. Food needs to be consumed in moderation—the right kinds of food in the right amounts so that we don't overeat ourselves into disease.

Lust of the Eyes. These are things that take root in the mind and soul of a person—inner greed, rage, jealousy, envy, pride. These are feelings of "I've got to have more...and more...and more." Lust of the eyes can lead to hate, anger, or rage at people who have what we want or what we think we deserve more than they do. A lust of the eyes is seeing anything that becomes an obsession or an all-consuming thought. These are the lusts of the *mind* and *heart* that lead to a *mental* or *emotional* stronghold that, *if acted upon*, will lead to a sin—theft, false witness against another person (including gossip, threats, defamation of character, and slander), covetousness, and even murder.

Self-denial is saying "no" to hateful, mean-spirited, greedy thoughts.

Is it wrong to desire nice things or to want the "good life"? Not at all! But our thinking about these things must be in the context of God's commandments, a spirit of love and generosity toward others, and a desire for *all* people around us to have nice things and live a "good life." We aren't to spent *any* of our money—not just God's portion, but *any* of our money—on obsessions or things aimed at hurting another person's property or life.

Pride of Life. This is a deeply rooted "I'm number one" spiritual attitude. This is the opposite of putting God first. This is denying the need for a spiritual life or the need to live in accordance with God's commandments. This is saying, "I don't need to tithe. I don't need to attend church. I don't need Jesus. I can make it on my own. I don't need to worship, I don't need to love, I don't need to obey."

The pride of life is basically a *spiritual* attitude that produces a *spiritual* separation from God.

Self-denial is ultimately saying "no" to pride.

Sacrifice and Self-Denial Are Part of "Surrender"

Sacrifice and self-denial are key ingredients of "surrender" to the Lord. Surrender isn't just "giving up," although it also that—a giving up of sinful behavior and sinful relationships, a giving up of old hurts and shame and guilt. God calls us to a total surrender. He calls us to sacrifice and to take up our cross *daily*.

The choices we make against the pride of life and the lust of the flesh and the lust of the eyes are choices we often face every day, and sometimes many times in a day. We must choose to follow Jesus. We must choose to keep God's commandments.

God calls us to surrender to Him our hearts, minds, and souls—and to do it with all our strength—everything we are and everything we have.

We will never know what God has for us until we surrender. It's only in "giving up" and "giving away" that we truly find ourselves! Right after Jesus said to take up our cross daily, He promised, *"For whosoever will save his life shall lose it: but whosoever will lose his life for my sake, the same shall save it. For what is a man advantaged, if he gain the whole world, and lose himself, or be cast away?"* (Luke 9:24–25)

I don't know what it is that you are required to give up in your personal life. I don't know the sins, old hurts, guilt, or shame of your past. I don't know what God is asking you specifically to give up when it comes to the pride in your life or the lust of your eyes or the lust of your flesh. The cross you are to take up daily is *your* cross. Jesus didn't say to take up *His* cross...He said to take up *your* cross. There are things that God wants to clean out of your life so you have room for the things He wants to put into your life!

I once watched a couple redecorate their living room and dining room. They carted out everything in those two rooms and took it to the dump. Then they took down the drapes, stripped the wallpaper, and took up the carpeting and took those items to the dump. Those rooms were empty, stripped of everything old.

They scrubbed those rooms, painted the walls, put down new flooring, hung new curtains at the window, and brought in all new furniture. It was a total transformation of those rooms.

That's what God has for you and me! He wants to clear out all of the old lusts and sins and pride and disobedience...all of the old guilt and shame and painful memories...all of the deep rage and anger and hatred and prejudice...and replace it with a *new life*. That new life is marked by new believing, new thinking, new emotions, new patterns of behavior, new habits. Sometimes it is marked by new friends and new relationships that are in accordance with God's commandments. It is marked by new devotion to God, new love for others, new habits of giving and obeying God.

Some of the old junk of your life needs to be cleared out to make room for the *new* blessings God has for you! You can't continue to cling to any of the old, worn-out, beat-up *stuff* of your life if you are going to have hands open to receive the new, just-right, beautiful, and lasting things that God has for you.

Read just a sampling from God's Word about the *new* things He has for you!

- *"Rejoice in the* LORD, *O ye righteous...sing unto him a new song...for the word of the* LORD *is right; and all his works are done in truth. He loveth righteousness and judgment: the earth is full of the goodness of the* LORD*"* (Psalm 33:1–4). God has a new *"song"* for the heart—a new attitude, a new and fresh outlook on life—for those who obey Him!

- *"They that wait upon the* LORD [serve Him] *shall renew their strength; they shall mount up with wings as eagles; they shall run, and not be weary; and they shall walk, and not faint"* (Isaiah 40:31). God has a new energy and vitality for those who obey Him!

- *"Remember ye not the former things, neither consider the things of old. Behold, I will do a new thing; now it shall spring forth; shall ye not know it? I will even make a way in the wilderness, and rivers in the desert"* (Isaiah 43:18–19). God has a new path—a new direction—and a total provision of refreshment for those who obey Him!

- *"Thou shalt be called by a new name, which the mouth of the* LORD *shall name"* (Isaiah 62:2). God has a new identity and reputation for those who obey Him!

- *"Cast away from you all your transgressions, whereby ye have transgressed; and make you a new heart and a new spirit"* (Ezekiel 18:31). God has a new freedom for the soul of those who obey Him!

- *"Therefore if any man be in Christ, he is a new creature: old things are passed away; behold, all things are become new"* (2 Corinthians 5:17). God has a brand-new *life*—spirit, mind, and soul—for the person who obeys Him!

Jesus taught:

No man putteth a piece of new cloth unto an old garment, for that which is put in to fill it up taketh from the garment, and the rent is made worse. Neither do men put new wine into old bottles: else the bottles break, and the wine runneth out, and the bottles perish: but they put new wine into new bottles, and both are preserved (Matthew 9:16–17).

Sacrifice and self-denial put us into obedience, and obedience to God results in God's *new things* being worked into our lives. Don't you want His "new work" in your life today? Don't you want His "new blessing" to be made manifest in you?

MAKE A COMMITMENT:
"I will follow God. I will live the life He has ordained for me. I will pursue a life of blessing, purity, and 'newness' in Christ Jesus."

Visit online at www.dennisleonardministries.com.

13

THE POWER OF A SEED

Have you ever known a person who was so smart he or she seemed to be a genius? But then, when you looked closely at that person's financial life, it seemed to be falling apart?

Have you ever known a person who seemed to have it "together" in his or her marriage relationship, but the person couldn't seem to make a dime to live on?

How can this be?

Because apart from God, there really isn't any true wisdom regarding the management of money and the creation of wealth. Without God, a person can "see and hear," but cannot truly understand the truth of God's Word, including the truth about giving and receiving. Faith, based upon a relationship with Jesus Christ, is the only means for people truly to receive into their mind and heart the truth that can set them on the road to financial freedom.

It is equally true that only a relationship with God can impart to a person the courage and ongoing determination that are necessary to obey God's commandments regarding giving. Only a relationship with

God can sustain people in their obedience and in their expressions of godly love.

Everything Begins with a Seed

One of the tremendous principles of God's Word is that everything related to life, growth, and multiplication begins with a *seed*.

If you want to see increase in your life, start planting "seed."

It is the seed that you plant that determines when, where, and how much your harvest will be. Some people think that because they pray about their needs all the time, at some point God will feel sorry for them and respond. No, God moves when you plant! He starts the growth of a harvest supply when your seed has been planted. I encourage you to study your Bible and learn everything you can about seed planting.

Cultivation of the Seed. Once a seed is in the ground and it begins to grow, that "crop" needs to be watered, weeded, and fertilized. Every farmer knows this. If the farmer just plants a seed and walks away, the harvest is going to be poor in quality and meager in quantity. The wise farmer plants a seed and then cultivates the plant that springs up.

The same is true for the financial seed we plant in the form of a tithe. We must water it, weed it, and fertilize it. This means that we must continually add doses of our faith to the seed we have planted. We need to root out any temptation to sin that might come as the devil's attempt to choke out the harvest God has planned for us. We need to stay in God's Word, meditate on it, and speak it frequently.

The better the care of the crop, the greater the harvest. That's true in both the natural and spiritual realms.

Wait for the "Due Season"

God promises a harvest "in due season." In the Old Testament, God gave this promise: *"I will give you rain in due season, and the land shall yield her increase, and the trees of the field shall yield their fruit"* (Leviticus 26:4). In the New Testament, the apostle Paul wrote, *"Let us not be weary in well doing: for in due season we shall reap, if we faint not"* (Galatians 6:9).

The Power of a Seed

Faith is what we hold onto while we're waiting for God to send the increase. Faith is what we "do" while we're waiting for God to grow our seed.

There is always a "waiting time" between the time a seed is planted and the harvest it produces. Tithing is not like an ATM machine in which you put your card and pull out money. Tithing is *planting*. It is sowing. The harvest will come, but in God's perfect timing.

Never Discount what God Counts

There are some people who say about their tithe, "My tithe is so small it can't possibly make a difference in the church. The church will never know if I don't tithe."

The church may not know, but God will.

Your tithe may be small, but in God's hands it's the beginning of a miracle harvest. Never discount what God counts. Huge trees grow from small seeds!

God's Word is filled with stories about people who gave "little seeds" and got back "big harvests." One of my favorite stories about giving and receiving is the story of a little widow and her son in Zarephath.

The prophet Elijah, who had been living out in the wilderness by the brook of Cherith, was told to go to Zarephath. This was during a time of tremendous drought and famine. God said to Elijah, *"I have commanded a widow woman there to sustain thee"* (1 Kings 17:9). Elijah did as God commanded.

When he got to Zarephath, Elijah met a widow woman at the gate of the city. He called to her and said, *"Fetch me, I pray thee, a little water in a vessel, that I may drink."* She did as he asked and then he said, *"Bring me, I pray thee, a morsel of bread in thine hand."* She said, *"As the LORD thy God liveth, I have not a cake, but an handful of meal in a barrel, and a little oil in a cruse: and, behold, I am gathering two sticks, that I may go in and dress it for me and my son, that we may eat it, and die"* (1 Kings 17:10–12).

Some people don't believe they have anything to give. The truth is, if you live on this earth, you have something to give! God will always provide a seed for the person willing to plant it! You may not have anything more than a few sticks, a handful of meal, and a little oil in a jar. With God, that's enough!

Elijah commanded the woman first to *"fear not."* That's very important. If fear rises up in you at the thought of giving what little you have, speak to that fear in the name of Jesus. Let your faith overcome your fear about giving.

Elijah then said, *"Go and do as thou hast said: but make me thereof a little cake first, and bring it unto me, and after make for thee and for thy son. For thus saith the LORD God of Israel, The barrel of meal shall not waste, neither shall the cruse of oil fail, until the day that the LORD sendeth rain upon the earth"* (1 Kings 17:13–14).

Elijah wanted this woman to get into firstfruits giving. He wanted her to give *first*. But he didn't ask her to give without also telling her God's promise about the harvest that God had ordained for her.

If you have very little to give, you especially need to understand the principle of *firstfruits* giving. You need to be planting a seed that God can grow. You need to be giving to God something for the Lord to multiply. God has a harvest set aside for you, but you must plant the seed to get that harvest supply moving in your direction.

The widow did what Elijah said and it came to pass just as Elijah had prophesied. *"The barrel of meal wasted not, neither did the cruse of oil fail, according to the word of the LORD"* (1 Kings 17:16). The Bible tells us that she and Elijah and *"her house"* did eat for many days! (See 1 Kings 17:15.)

Timeless principles from God's Word are found in this passage:

1. When you give to God first, He makes things *last*.

2. Wilderness giving gets you out of wilderness living.

3. God knows your fate, but He is moved by your *faith*.

4. Life's troubles can be the soil in which you need to dig to uncover God's treasures.

Make a decision today that you are going to be faithful in your giving, regardless of the amount of your giving.

The Power of a Seed

God Produces the Harvest

No person can multiply a seed. Only God can cause this multiplication process. He is the one who brings it about.

Giving always makes me excited because when I see people give, I also see them become "wealth magnets." Money and opportunities and ideas about investing and starting businesses just seem to flow toward them.

A person might be seated at a conference table with twelve other people...and his project is the one that is approved.

A person's loan application might be one of five hundred...but hers is the application that surfaces and is approved first.

A person discovers that the lights all seem to turn green...he feels as if he's at the "right place at the right time"...he meets just the people he needs to meet to get the information he needs to have to turn a dream into a reality.

A Continual Harvest. A person who gets into a rhythm of frequent giving is a person who puts himself into position to receive almost a continual harvest. Harvest after harvest...comes from giving after giving. To live in continual harvest, get into continual giving!

An ongoing rhythm of giving and receiving is one of the earliest promises in God's Word: *"While the earth remaineth, seedtime and harvest, and cold and heat, and summer and winter, and day and night shall not cease"* (Genesis 8:22). A harvest following seedtime is a *sure deal* in God's economy.

No banker can promise you a sure harvest all the time.

No stock broker can make a promise that all stocks will rise in value.

No real estate broker can ensure that real estate will always continue to go up like a rocket.

Only God's promise of seedtime and harvest is an ongoing all-the-time *certainty.*

It's easy to get in a regular habit of seedtime when things seem to go well. It's a challenge when adversity strikes. It's then, however, that you need to dig in your heels and refuse to stop planting. The harvest *will come.*

A Whole-Life Harvest. God's harvest back to you covers your entire life. I don't know the nature of the *full* harvest you will receive from your obedience in faithful tithing, but I do know this:

Money is a harvest.

A good medical report is a harvest.

Favor among your co-workers and neighbors is a harvest.

Peace in your heart is a harvest.

Your harvest involves everything that is good and pure and eternal in your life. It involves everything that is good and pure and delightful in this present time. God knows what you need and He supplies it...in abundance.

MAKE A COMMITMENT:
"I will plant my seed and I *will* reap
the harvest God grows!"

14

ACTIVATE YOUR FAITH
WHEN YOU GIVE

*F*aith seems to be a rather nebulous term to many people. They don't understand what faith is because it isn't something they can see, touch, or feel. It's a "spiritual" term that we hear often, but many people have trouble defining faith.

Faith is simply trusting God to do what He said He would do.

It doesn't mean trusting God to do what *you* necessarily want Him to do. It means trusting God to do what *He* has said in His Word He wants to do, is doing, and will do.

Faith is choosing to obey God...and then trusting Him with the consequences. It is living according to God's commandments, speaking what God says to speak, giving what God says to give, and doing what God says to do...regardless of what others say, give, do, or tell *you* to say, give, or do.

How we live our life is a sign of our faith—both to people around us and to God. Faith isn't just what we believe; it's how we express our belief in all we *do*.

Faith and giving are like the two oars of a rowboat. If you use only one oar, you go in circles. You must use both oars to get anywhere. James 2:26 says, *"For as the body without the spirit is dead, so faith without works is dead also."*

Don't just toss your offering or tithe into the basket as it goes by. Activate your faith as you give! Pray as you write out your tithe check:

"God, this check represents my faith in You and Your ability to work miracles and bring supernatural breakthroughs in my life and in my family. This is how much I believe in You and Your supernatural ability. I have faith that You can make a way for me. Even though it looks as if I can't afford to write this check, I do it anyway!"

Put your gift into the offering basket with boldness. Start expecting God to be at work in you and on your behalf.

God's Word says that we may cast our bread on the waters, but after many days that bread will come back to us (Ecclesiastes 11:1). You never lose anything you plant in the kingdom of God!

When you give your tithe, you are expressing your faith. Speak out of your faith for *all* that you need, not just the finances you need:

- "God, I give You this sacrificial offering and I am believing You to save my child."

- "God, I am trusting You with my tithe and I am believing for You to save my spouse."

- "God, I am giving to You as You commanded. I am trusting You to command all things in my life to turn for good. I know my loved one may be guilty as charged, but I believe You will deliver him."

Create an Upward Spiral of Believing and Giving

Every time you give of your finances to God, renew your faith commitment to God! Start believing God to be true to His end of His agreement with you. Start looking for the blessings to come into your life. The more you believe God, the more your "expectancy" moves to a new level.

Activate Your Faith When You Give

Believe God...give to God...and inevitably you'll find that God is faithful to bless you. As He begins to bless you, you'll find that you believe in God even more! You'll be more eager to give to God with a renewed, yes, even explosive faith, and as you give with faith, you'll find that God is faithful to bless you with greater blessings. It's an upward cycle. Believing...giving...receiving the blessing... believing...giving...receiving the blessing...believing...and so forth. Your faith will grow. Your giving will grow. Your receiving—your harvest of blessings—will grow. Which will only cause your faith to grow!

Life gets better...and better...and better. The trend is an upward trend.

That doesn't mean there may not be small glitches along the way. That doesn't mean every relationship will be totally smooth sailing or that everything you touch will turn to gold. It doesn't mean you won't face some difficulties. Troubles, trials, and turbulence are a part of life. The good news in the face of those troubles is this: God's blessings will sustain you through the trials. God's favor remains on your life. And the upward trend in your life will continue. You won't be five years from now where you are today. You won't be ten years from now where you will be five years from now!

Real faith says, "I have it now. I just can't see it yet."

Real faith says, "It already is according to God's Word."

Real faith says, "By His stripes I'm already healed."

Real faith says, "My entire household shall be saved."

Real faith anticipates and says what *God* declares to be His truth, His will, His desire.

Your reward is tied to your faith. Hebrews 11:6 says, *"But without faith it is impossible to please him: for he that cometh to God must believe that he is, and that he is a rewarder of them that diligently seek him."* Believe God to be *your* rewarder!

Stay "Tuned In" for God's Rewards

Some people miss God's will for their life because they have to figure out everything ahead of time. "How will God save my spouse?" "How will God get me a car?" "How will God increase my income?" Stop worrying about *how* God will work. He has more ways than you can imagine. You can't ever fully figure out all that God has in mind for you!

Put your faith and giving together and keep expecting results. Stay on the alert for them.

The truth is, God specializes in taking nothing and making something out of it. That's what He does with every broken person who comes to Him with a humble heart to receive His offer of forgiveness and eternal life. That's what He does with sick bodies. That's what He does with bankrupt finances. Give what you have to God and watch Him work! Let me remind you of this incident in the New Testament:

And when it was evening, his disciples came to him, saying, This is a desert place, and the time is now past; send the multitude away, that they may go into the villages, and buy themselves victuals [food to eat]. But Jesus said unto them, They need not depart; give ye them to eat. And they say unto him, We have here but five loaves, and two fishes. He said, Bring them hither to me. And he commanded the multitude to sit down on the grass, and took the five loaves, and the two fishes, and looking up to heaven, he blessed, and brake, and gave the loaves to his disciples, and the disciples to the multitude. And they did all eat, and were filled: and they took up of the fragments that remained twelve baskets full. And they that had eaten were about five thousand men, beside women and children (Matthew 14:15–21).

Circumstances said there was no food for the people on this hillside in the Galilee region. The situation was one of hunger. But then, one young boy was willing to give what he had to God. And the result was the gift given into the hands of Jesus became food for thousands to be fed and blessed! And not only that, but there were twelve baskets of leftovers—one basket for each of the disciples to eat! What a tremendous harvest!

Be Like David!

One of the best examples of faith in action in the Bible is David's response to a devastating blow he and his followers experienced while they lived in Ziklag. David and his four hundred men had gone to offer their services to Achish, who had assisted David in the past. Achish was grateful for their offer of military assistance but his other allies refused their participation and David and his men were sent home. When they returned to Ziklag, they discovered that the city had been burned and all the women and children had been carried away as captives. The Bible tells us that *"David and the people that were with him lifted up their voice and wept, until they had no more power to weep"* (1 Samuel 30:4).

The men were so distraught in their grief they even spoke of stoning David. In addition, there seems to have been some confusion about which way the invading Amalekites had gone, how many were in the raiding party, or whether the Lord desired for them to go in pursuit of what had been taken from them.

David did two things. First, he *"encouraged himself in the LORD his God"* (1 Samuel 30:6). This means that David began to sing and praise God. Let me assure you of this—singing and praising God *always* rekindle a person's faith. You can't sing praises to God without reminding your own soul of God's greatness, His faithfulness, His trustworthiness, and His generosity toward you. You can't shout praises to God without reminding your own heart and mind of God's power, wisdom, love, and majesty. The more you praise God with a pure and genuine intent of honoring God and acknowledging Him in your life, the more your faith is going to rise up in you.

Words of praise become words of faith. It's only one very small step from saying, "I praise You, Lord, for Your absolute trustworthiness" to saying, "I trust You, Lord—I trust You with my whole life!" What you believe about God *is* faith. What you voice about God becomes your statement of faith.

If you want to get God's attention, you have to speak faith, even if everything around you seems impossible.

The more David encouraged himself in the Lord, the stronger he became. The more he used his faith, the more he felt motivated to take action.

Faith should always motivate you to take action. Faith isn't intended just for verbal praise and a feel-good attitude inside you. Faith is intended to be put to use.

God's plan for you is that you succeed. His plan is always a "victory" plan. It's the specifics related to that plan that you are required to pursue with your faith.

Your faith should motivate you to seek the Lord until you know where the success and victory lie! God has a plan for your success. He has a plan for your financial freedom. The plan He has for you is unique—it may not at all be the same specific plan He has for the person who sits next to you in church or who lives next to you in your neighborhood.

The second thing David did was to inquire of the Lord about what God wanted him to *do*. He asked the Lord, *"Shall I pursue after this troop? shall I overtake them?"* The Lord replied, *"Pursue: for thou shalt surely overtake them, and without fail recover all"* (1 Samuel 30:8).

In asking the Lord, "Shall I pursue?" David was really asking, "Shall I pursue them *now*?" Timing is important. David knew that God wanted him to regain his two wives, their children, and the possessions that had been stolen from him. He knew God wanted his men to have their families and possessions restored. It was a matter of when, how, where, and what course of action to take.

Faith will speak to you, "God desires for you to live in financial freedom."

Faith will speak to you, "God desires for you to be the head and not the tail."

Faith will speak to you, "God desires for you to succeed in what you put your hand to."

Faith will speak to you, "God desires for you to multiply and to experience a hundred-fold return."

Your inquiry to God is not, "God, do You want to bless me?" but rather, "God, is now the time...is this the direction...is this the plan...is this the 'how' and 'where' and 'when' You have in mind?"

God replied to David, "Pursue. You will recover all."

David didn't know it at the time God spoke this, but God had a different meaning of *"all"* than David probably had. David pursued the Amalekites expecting to get back all that had been stolen from him. God had in mind *more* than that.

As David pursued the Amalekites, God gave him a brilliant battle plan. He allowed David and his men to come across a young Egyptian, a former servant to one of the Amalekites, who had become ill. This man told David precisely where the Amalekites had gone. David and two hundred of his four hundred men took the Amalekites by surprise and, indeed, they recovered all that the Amalekites had carried away—all the wives, sons, daughters, and possessions that had been taken.

But then the Bible tells us, *"David took all the flocks and the herds, which they drave before those other cattle, and said, This is David's spoil"* (1 Samuel 30:20). In other words, David took everything that the Amalekites had captured out of the land of the Philistines and out of the land of Judah. It wasn't just what had been taken from Ziklag, but what the Amalekites had taken out of all the other towns and camps they had raided!

It was this spoil that David used to gain great support from the elders of Judah. He said to his friends, *"Behold a present for you of the spoil of the enemies of the LORD"* (1 Samuel 30:26).

It was only a matter of days later that David got word of King Saul's death. His victory and recovery of *"all"*—and his giving of presents to the elders of Judah—set David up to be named king of Judah. With Ziklag in ashes, David and his men and their families had nothing to draw them back to Ziklag. They were willing to move—and they did move—to Hebron. There, David reigned as king for seven years before moving to Jerusalem and becoming king over the entire nation of Israel.

Yes, God's plan for David was a plan for a mighty victory, tremendous success, and awesome financial gain.

Put your faith into motion! Encourage yourself in the Lord. Inquire of the Lord as to His specific plan for you. And then *pursue* what God reveals to you. Go for it with your entire being. Expect to gain all that God has purposed in your heart...and more!

MAKE A COMMITMENT:
"I will wrap my tithe in faith!
I will give and believe
and give and believe and give and
believe and give and…"

Visit online at www.dennisleonardministries.com.

15

FILL YOUR HEART WITH LOVE

The motive for giving is not receiving money. God's blessings are not the "reason" to give. No—it's not about the harvest or the reward. It's not even about the fact that we are commanded to give.

No...the reason we give is because we love.

"God so loved...that he gave."

We so love...that we give.

The most famous verse in the New Testament spells it out: *"For God so loved the world, that he gave his only begotten Son, that whosoever believeth in him should not perish, but have everlasting life"* (John 3:16).

When it comes to sacrificial giving, nobody sacrificed in giving more than God. Nobody gave more than God gave, with greater love, or greater belief in a tremendous harvest. *"For God so loved the world, that he gave his only begotten Son, that whosoever believeth in him should not perish, but have everlasting life"* (John 3:16).

God so loved.

God gave.

God believed in the harvest of your soul and mind so that we might live with Him forever.

Salvation is free because of the tremendously high price Jesus paid on the cross...the cost of His sinless, perfect life.

The Great Commandments—They're All about Love!

"Love" is the supreme commandment. Jesus once was asked to identify the greatest commandments. He said,

> And thou shalt love the Lord thy God with all thy heart, and with all thy soul, and with all thy mind, and with all thy strength: this is the first commandment. And the second is like, namely this, Thou shalt love thy neighbour as thyself. There is none other commandment greater than these (Mark 12:30–31).

The first great commandment is to "love God" and to do so with all our soul, mind, and strength.

How do we do this?

One way is to recall continually to our own minds all that God has done for us and to thank Him for His many blessings.

Three Lists. I strongly encourage you to keep track of three things. Get yourself a little journal or a small ledger for just this purpose. Write down your giving. Make your entries with joy. I call this a "List of Giving."

Then write down the things you are believing God to do on your behalf. These are not just your prayer requests for current "needs" in your life or the lives of others, but also your goals and your dreams. I call this a "List of Desires."

And then, write down the blessings that come your way. List those things for which you give thanks and praise. Document the goodness of God in your life. Ask the Lord to open your eyes so you can take in more and more of what it is He is doing for you and ha done for you in the past. Make this your ongoing "List of Blessings."

122

Fill Your Heart with Love

Thank God daily for His provision, His protection, and the many "harvests" He has sent your way. This is one great way to show love to God.

Praise God for all He is. You can never reach the end of praising God for His attributes because God is infinite!

Beyond thanksgiving and praising, your giving is a way of expressing love to God.

"I love the Lord," people tell me. "I just don't tithe."

If you love the Lord you will tithe. You will *want* to obey the one you love. You will *want* to serve Him and keep His commandments.

Jesus made this very clear. He said three times in the fourteenth chapter of the Gospel of John, "If you love Me, you will keep My commandments." (See John 14:21, 23, 24.) The commandments include the commandments to give.

The second great commandment of Jesus was to love others as we love ourselves. This is the message throughout the New Testament, as well as through the law of the Old Testament. As Christians we are commanded to care for one another and to walk in love. Read Philippians 2:2–5:

> *Fulfil ye my joy, that ye be likeminded, having the same love, being of one accord, of one mind. Let nothing be done through strife or vainglory; but in lowliness of mind let each esteem other better than themselves. Look not every man on his own things, but every man also on the things of others. Let this mind be in you, which was also in Christ Jesus.*

God's Word mandates that Christians "cover" one another—we are to be there for one another, to build up one another, to share a mutual life in Christ. This does not mean we are to lie for one another, but rather, we are to speak truth to one another. We are to encourage and admonish and counsel and edify one another.

Most people treat themselves very well. In fact, if a person doesn't care for himself we say that he is mentally ill or demented. So, if you love others as you love yourself, you will give to others without reservation and seek to "care" for others in generous, loving ways. You will give consideration to those around you, including your family members, neighbors, co-workers, and yes, even your enemies. Jesus taught:

> But love ye your enemies, and do good, and lend, hoping for nothing again; and your reward shall be great, and ye shall be the children of the Highest: for he is king unto the unthankful and to the evil. Be ye therefore merciful, as your Father also is merciful (Luke 6:35–36).

Why does the Bible tell us to give and show love to our enemies? The path toward God is paved with mercy, kindness, and patience. If we have a relationship with God, then we need to rid ourselves of the desire for revenge. We need to remove bitterness and anger from our hearts. One way is to give—for there's something about giving that brings healing to our hearts. This especially seems to be true when we give to those whom we don't particularly like or whom we believe have harmed us in some way.

The Bible Portrait of Love. The Bible gives us of a portrait of what godly love looks like:

- Love is being willing to give your life for someone else (John 15:13).
- Love is treating others as well as you treat yourself (Romans 13:9).
- Love is doing no evil to your fellow man (Romans 13:10).
- Love is living without fear. (1 John 4:18).
- Love is keeping God's commandments (2 John 6).
- Love is being not envious, prideful, or rude, but rather, being patient and kind, loving truth and always believing the best (1 Corinthians 13:4–7).

Love is a *verb*. It is active. It's expressed in doing and giving. If you find it difficult to show love, simply start where you are.

"Well," you may be saying, "to whom can I give love?"

There are countless people all around you who need your love. One of the best ways to start showing love is to volunteer to be part of a group that is giving to others in need—perhaps a team of people who is feeding the homeless or gathering and cleaning clothes for poor children. Volunteer at food bank. Visit hospitals or nursing homes. Visit those who are homebound. Go to a children's hospital or a homeless shelter and see what you can do to help. Become a team player in the volunteer ministry in which you work. Choose to be flexible, generous, and easy to get along with.

Here are other ideas:

- Give away those clothes in your closet that you don't wear anymore.

- Quit trying to sell your old furniture and bless someone with a gift of it.

- Watch out for your neighbors and their home. Volunteer to pick up their paper or mail while they are away on vacation.

- Help people on your job.

As you position yourself in a lifestyle of giving, you will find you have more happiness and peace. Stingy people live miserable lives. Don't be like Mr. Scrooge in *A Christmas Carol*—he lived a tortured life until he started to give.

There are two main inland bodies of water in Israel. The northern body of water is the Sea of Galilee. The southern is the Dead Sea. They are connected by the Jordan River.

The Sea of Galilee is a beautiful body of water that receives water from three sources and gives out water. The two processes happen every day, simultaneously. The Sea of Galilee is alive with an abundance of fish.

The Dead Sea, on the other hand, receives water but doesn't give any water out. As a result, it is stagnant. It is filled with minerals, but not *life*.

This is a wonderful picture of our giving. Those who give out continuously are filled with *life*. Those who don't give are stagnant. What you give out in love always comes back to you in an enlarged capacity to love. With love comes life!

A harvest of blessings includes love. When you give love, you receive love in return—not necessarily from the person to whom you give love, but love from people nonetheless. If you give your time and resources, you receive back time and resources. What you sow is what you reap.

Loving and Giving to the World. Jesus told us very specifically what we were to give to the world as a whole. He said, *"Heal the sick, cleanse the lepers, raise the dead, cast out devils: freely ye have received, freely give"* (Matthew 10:8).

The *"sick"* include any who have an area of weakness, disease, injury, or wound in their lives—emotional, physical, spiritual. We all are sick in some way.

The *"lepers"* are those who are considered to be social outcasts—very often the people in prison, the poor, and people of various racial backgrounds or educational deficiencies. We all are an "outcast" from *some* group of people!

The *"dead"* we are to raise are primarily those who are dead in their sins and trespasses. They are the ones who have no hope, no eternal life, no Holy Spirit within them. We all feel "dead on our feet" at times. We all sin.

The *"cast[ing] out of devils"* includes the release of people from all oppression and influence of demonic powers, as well as casting demons out of people who are truly demon possessed. The truth is, we all are tempted and oppressed by the devil from time to time.

There are plenty of people all around you who need for you to *freely* and generously give what you have freely and generously received from the Lord. In areas where you are experiencing the strength and wisdom of the Lord, freely give that strength and wisdom to those who are weak and moving in error.

Give...because in the end, you too will have need.

If you need money...give money.

If you need love...give love.

If you need more time...give of your time.

If you need forgiveness...give forgiveness.

And who among us doesn't have these needs? We all do!

The law of sowing and reaping is all about loving others as we love ourselves.

Fill Your Heart with Love

Forgiveness Is an Act of Love

Let me remind you again of John 3:16: *"For God so loved the world, that he gave his only begotten Son, that whosoever believeth in him should not perish, but have everlasting life."*

God so loved...that God gave the provision that would result in the *forgiveness* of sin. What God has given to us—His forgiveness—we must give to others.

Make a decision to forgive others as an act of your love. It is *as* you forgive others that God forgives you. Don't take any chances of being cursed because of unforgiveness in your heart. None of us knows how much time we have left on this earth—the Bible refers to life as a *"vapor"* that quickly passes away. If the next five minutes were the last five minutes of your life on this earth, wouldn't you want to know with certainty that you had God's forgiveness, that you had forgiven anyone who had wronged you, and that you had asked for forgiveness from those you had wronged? The only way to die in peace is to know that you are forgiven and that you have forgiven others.

What did the Lord say He would do on behalf of those who would do this? Read His words and be encouraged!

> Be glad and rejoice, for the LORD will do great things...he hath given you the former rain moderately, and he will cause to come down for you the rain, the former rain, and the latter rain in the first month. And the floors shall be full of wheat, and the fats shall overflow with wine and oil. And I will restore to you the years that the locust hath eaten, the cankerworm, and the caterpillar, and the palmerworm...And ye shall eat in plenty, and be satisfied, and praise the name of the LORD your God, that hath dealt wondrously with you: and my people shall never be ashamed (Joel 2:21–26).

Do you remember the story of Job? He was a man who loved God but lost his family and all his wealth. His friends came to question him yet, in the aftermath of all they said to him, Job declared that he trusted God. He forgave those around him. And God gave him *double* what he had before. (See Job 42:10.)

127

Ask yourself today, "Is there someone I need to forgive?" Do you have "issues" with people round you? Are you at odds with your boss, your neighbor, or your pastor? Your life today may be bound up emotionally because you are holding a grudge against your ex-spouse, a child, your supervisor at work, or a "former friend." In order to become free inside you are going to have to forgive those who have hurt you, disappointed you, or abandoned you.

Remember always that Jesus taught, *"If ye do not forgive, neither will your Father which is in heaven forgive your trespasses"* (Mark 11:26). Even if a person has wronged you in a thousand ways, or so deeply that you think the trespass can never be forgiven, ask God to help you forgive. You *must* forgive to be fully forgiven by your heavenly Father. I invite you to pray this prayer:

"Dear Lord, I confess that I have allowed unforgiveness to take root in my heart. I am now willing to let it go. Please help me to forgive every person who has harmed me. I ask You to replace my anger and resentment with peace, joy, and love. By faith I receive the peace of God in my heart. In Jesus' name I pray, amen."

To get out of the emotional desert in which you have been wandering and to start experiencing the fullness of living in God's promised land...you must forgive.

One of the greatest acts of forgiveness you can make is to pray for the person who has hurt you. Ask God to do His work in them. Then trust Him to do it!

Love and Forgiveness Set You Free to Move Forward

Love and forgiveness free you from the bonds of hatred, anger, bitterness, and revenge. They set you free to move forward into a new way of living, a new harvest, a new life!

The time has come for many Christians today to close certain chapters in their life and allow God to write some new chapters!

The past is the past. It is *over.* So many people live today with yesterday guiding their lives. It is time to move forward into today and tomorrow.

Fill Your Heart with Love

If you will sell out to the Lord, He will show you how to bring increase into your life. He will teach you how to make money. He will give you creative ideas and implementation strategies. I have seen God put people into jobs they weren't qualified to have, and then teach them how to accomplish the tasks with supernatural wisdom.

You are a representative of God on this earth. It pleases Him when people see His blueprint all over your life. Let them wonder how you can accomplish so much with so little. Let them call you lucky. You know the source of your accomplishment. You know that it isn't luck at all, but *God Almighty*, who is displaying Himself and His power, wisdom, and love through your life.

Close the Door on the Past and Open the Door to Your Future

You may be hurting because of abuse in your childhood.

You may be suffering because of hurtful criticism or rejection in your past.

You may be reeling from an unexpected blow.

You may be discouraged because of things you've gone through recently.

You have to be willing to walk away from your past. That takes courage. It may mean walking away from someone you know is not God's will for you to have as a friend or a business associate. It may mean walking away from a job that you know is not God's will for you—especially if that job promotes sin or is conducive to an immoral, ungodly lifestyle. It may mean giving up something that you know is not God's will for you to have or to practice. Be willing to say "no" to that chemical addiction, that dependency on an abusive person, that dabbling in the occult.

You also need to give up your tears over that person who left you or that business failure you experienced or the injustice that was leveled at you. Refuse to hold on to the pain of rejection, criticism, or ridicule. Wipe your eyes, lift up your head, start praising God, and walk into your future. Let God take you to a new place in Him!

You also have to be willing to open yourself up to the future God has for you. Start telling yourself the truth:

• "My best days are *ahead* of me, not behind me."

- *"No weapon...formed against* [me] *shall prosper"* (Isaiah 54:17).

- "God forgives, and what God forgives I must forgive."

- "God has a better idea!"

- "No matter what the enemy has done to harm me, God can turn it to my good." (See Genesis 50:20.)

- "This drought may have lasted a long time but an abundance of rain is coming my way!"

You may need to preach the truth of God's Word to yourself in the bathroom mirror.

You may need to preach the truth of God's Word to yourself with tears running down your face.

You may need to preach the truth of God's Word to yourself in the dark of your own bedroom when you are all alone and sacred.

If that's the case, preach on!

Speak out words of faith. Keep acting in obedience to God's commands. Keep giving. Remind God of His promises and remind yourself of His faithfulness in keeping those promises, not only to people in Bible times but also to you in the past times of your own life. You didn't survive to this day without miracles from God at work *on your behalf.* You don't have the health, abilities, skills, insights, faith, or anything else in your life that you have without the miracle-working power of God at work *on your behalf.*

Refuse to judge your future by your past. Bury your past and let God resurrect your future.

Don't keep harping to God about how big the giants are in your life. Start telling your giants how big God is!

Look for God's new thing in your life...starting today! Read again God's promise to you, *"Remember ye not the former things, neither consider the things of old. Behold, I will do a new thing; now it shall spring forth; shall ye not know it? I will even make a way in the wilderness, and rivers in the desert"* (Isaiah 43:18–19).

MAKE A COMMITMENT:
"I will walk in love. I will forgive.
I will move forward in my life!"

16

THREE PRACTICAL ESSENTIALS: DESIRE, DISCIPLINE, AND DETERMINATION

In addition to faith, love, and forgiveness, there are three things you must have if you truly are going to change the overall direction of your life: desire, discipline, and determination. These three essentials go hand in hand.

Essential #1: Desire

You've got to *want* to change.

Many people *say* they want to change but they don't really want to get rid of old familiar patterns. They don't want to walk away from sin. They don't want to give up relationships that they know are destructive. They're in a rut and they might daydream about getting out of that rut, but they aren't willing to make any effort toward that goal.

How much do you really desire a *change*? How much do you desire to move beyond your current position in life?

Desire is more than a simple ol' wish or a happy li'l hope. It's more than a fantasy or whim. A desire is a deep longing. It's like a craving—it compels something deep within you to begin to move. A desire has a "consuming" quality to it—it captures your imagination, fills your thoughts, warms your heart, and prods you to respond to it. You can't walk away from a genuine desire. A desire demands your attention.

Because a desire has this "deep longing" or "passionate" quality to it, it's vitally important that the things you desire be in keeping with God's desire for you.

Is it wrong for you to desire to marry a man you deeply love? No...as long as that man isn't already married to someone else! It *is* wrong for you to have a desire for someone else's husband!

Is it wrong for you to desire to feel healthy and vibrant and have great energy? No. But it is wrong to turn to cocaine or crack to get a "high."

Is it wrong for you to desire to have nice things and to go on fun family vacations? No. But it is wrong to steal nice things from someone else. It is wrong to kidnap children and run away with them and call yourselves a family on a vacation!

You get the picture.

Is it wrong for you to have a lot of money? No. It's wrong only if you gain that money in an illegal or immoral, ungodly way. It's wrong only if you hoard that money and don't do anything with it to bless others. It's wrong only if you keep all that money for yourself and fail to trust God with it and fail to obey His commandments about the giving of tithes and offerings.

Make sure your desires are in line with God's Word. If you have questions about whether they are in line, ask a godly counselor or a pastor.

The problem I see most often is not that people have wrong desires, but that they don't have *any* deep desires about their own improvement. They are opting for a truly lackluster existence. They just take life as it comes, one day after the next, dealing with one problem after the next. They don't have God-given dreams for their life. They aren't pressing toward a goal. They're in "idle" mode—the engine is running and they're burning up gas, but they aren't going anywhere!

If you don't have deep desire for something *more* in your life, ask God what He desires for you. Be open to His answer. I guarantee you that the Lord desires more for you than you presently have. Get a glimpse into His goals and dreams for you. Choose to adopt God's vision for your life and to make His desire your desire.

Getting in Shape. God's way of giving is like an exercise routine. Just as with any workout, the more you do it, the easier it gets. It becomes automatic. It becomes rhythmic.

Initially it hurts to get into shape. Everybody who has worked out in a gym knows the old motto "no pain, no gain." It takes effort and intention to toughen up physically. The same is true for tithing. If you haven't tithed, you may feel that tithing "hurts" initially. However, the more you exercise physically, the more you discover that eventually it "hurts" *not* to exercise—you feel worse when you *don't exercise*. This is absolutely the same in tithing. You will find that if you don't tithe, the pain is greater than when you do.

The real question is this: "Do you want to stay in the shape you're in?"

The great motivation for physical exercise lies in the answer to the question, "Do you want to stay in the physical shape you're in?" The great motivation for financial freedom lies in the answer to the question, "Do you want to stay in the financial shape you're in?" And the great motivation spiritually lies in the question, "Do you want to stay in the same spiritual rut you're in—or do you desire to grow, mature, and become spiritually strong and effective in ways you presently aren't?"

Essential #2: Discipline

One of the major concepts related to discipline is found in this two-word phrase: "first thing."

Have you ever tried to develop a strong prayer life? You know that it takes discipline to pray daily, day after day, week after week, year after year. I'm not talking about a quick little prayer here or there through the day or an occasional "Help me, God" or "Praise You, Lord" prayer. I'm talking about serious time set aside for diligent thanksgiving, praising, petitioning, and interceding. That kind of prayer requires discipline. It means setting aside time in your schedule and making that alone-time with God a priority.

The easiest way I know to adopt a discipline of prayer is to make a decision to pray "first thing." First thing in the morning, spend time with the Lord. Talk to God, voicing all of your concerns, feelings, and needs to Him. I suggest you pray with your Bible open on your lap. Get God's opinions. Let Him guide your reading. Listen as much or more than you talk. Make prayer the "first thing" you do in your day.

And then, before you have a major appointment or go into a meeting, make prayer the "first thing" you do—the first thing in the meeting, especially if it is a meeting related to the ministry of the church or if it's a meeting with other Christians. If you are going into

God's Way Works!

"When my husband I married, we had three credit cards between us with a total balance of more than nine thousand dollars! We were young professionals making a combined income of about seventy-eight thousand dollars. That sounds like a lot, but it really wasn't given our bills and our dreams. We found it hard to think about giving away money when were trying to pay off our credit cards and raise the down payment for a house.

"Finally we stepped out in faith. We sacrificed and paid our tithes and offerings consistently—no matter what. Giving our tithe meant saying 'no' to some things we really wanted to own or to do, but we said 'no' anyway. We cut out all the 'extras.' We took our lunches to work, went out for dinner only on special occasions, and held onto our older cars instead of buying new ones.

"It wasn't easy, but as we remained faithful we eventually paid off our debt. We contracted our first house to be built and moved in, with God miraculously providing a lender who required that we only put down ten percent on the house. God also blessed me with a new job that allowed me to earn ten thousand dollars a year more than I had previously been making. Not only that, but this new job allowed me to remain home—in my previous job I had to travel for weeks at a time. **(continued)** an appointment or meeting with an unbeliever, you really need to make prayer the "first thing" you do before you walk into that appointment or conference room.

Think about exercise. The best time of day for exercise is "first thing in the morning." Now you can't have two "first things"—or can you? I know a number of people who pray while they walk or jog or ride a stationery bike. They pour out their hearts to God even as sweat pours from their body! People who are serious about physical fitness have told me on numerous occasions that if they don't exercise "first thing" in the morning, they never seem to find time to get around to it.

Others have told me that exercise is the "first thing" they do when they get home from work in the afternoon. They lace on their shoes and go for a walk, which really helps them unwind from the

God's Way Works!

"Shortly after I got my new job, my husband's company announced plans to spin off his division and close the location where he worked. God showed his favor upon my husband and he was invited to transfer—all expenses paid. Our home was purchased by the company with enough left over for a *greater* down payment on a new house. Even before we moved, God blessed me with a job in our new location. He allowed us to purchase a brand-new home that was larger and nicer than the one we'd just built. It was located only minutes from my husband's job. In his previous job he had a long commute. We were grateful for the added hours we could be together!

"God has been so good. Over the years we have maintained our tithe, increased our offerings, and still been able to cover all of our increased living and childcare expenses. We have been able to pay off student loans, put some money away in savings, and *still* have enough money for some 'extras.' We have survived two layoffs and many other difficulties in recent years.

"Both my husband and I firmly believe that we have been blessed so royally because we tithe. We are committed to each other and to our marriage and family, but most of all, we are committed to the Lord and to being obedient to His Word." — Yolanda workday so they are in a better mood and have more energy for their families in the evening. One woman told me that exercising for twenty minutes is the "first thing" she does during her lunch hour. Actually, it's the only thing she does during her lunch hour besides drink a protein drink.

Adopt a "first thing" policy and discipline seems to follow.

Now what does this have to do with tithing? Everything! The Bible refers to the tithe as *first*fruits. Tithing is the "first thing" we are to do with income we receive.

In very practical terms, when that paycheck is in your hand and is deposited into the bank or cashed, the first check you write or the first portion of money you set aside in an envelope is the ten percent that goes to the storehouse of the Lord. It's the *first* money you spend.

If you wait until later in the month to see if you have "enough left over" to tithe, I can almost guarantee you that you will never have enough left over. In fact, you aren't likely to have anything left over!

It takes faith to set aside the *first* ten percent and give it. It takes ongoing faith and *discipline* to continue to tithe regularly and faithfully.

The moment you give that ten percent to God, God's blessing is immediately stamped on the other ninety percent. It's truly amazing to see what God does to stretch and multiply that money. I've seen it happen over and over again—people seem to have *more* money after they tithe than they did before they got into the discipline of tithing.

Three major things seem to happen to tithers as they begin to spend the ninety percent that is theirs.

More Intentional Spending. One thing that seems to happen is tithers become much more intentional about when and for what the ninety percent is spent. There's more thought behind a tither's spending habits.

People often get into trouble with money because they don't think about what they're spending. They buy "on impulse." They get a craving for an item and rush right out and buy it as soon as they have a little money or a new credit card. They don't take time to think about the purchase, to weigh if the item is the *best* item to buy, or to discuss with wise counselors if the purchase is a wise use of their money. Rather, they want what they want and they buy it when they want it, regardless of whether they can pay for it. The end result is often debt or spending that is out of control.

If people think about what they are buying, they tend to comparison shop. They tend to wait until they can get the most quality for the least price—they are more willing to wait for a top-of-the-line item to go on sale, or to wait for their dream car to hit the used-car market rather than spend money for a new car that quickly depreciates in value. They look at price tags and think about them. The end result is less debt and no out-of-control credit accounts.

More Diligent in Money Management. The second thing that I've seen in tithers is that they are more diligent in the way they deal with the ninety percent that is theirs. They make budgets to ensure that the necessary bills are paid in full *before* they spend money for things that are purely for pleasure.

Much Smarter in Investing. The third thing that I've seen in tithers is that, given their more intentional approach to spending and their greater inclination to make a budget, they are much more likely to think about long-range financial goals. They aren't living in the moment when it comes to their spending. They plan more. And as part of those plans, they are much more likely to include some spending that goes into a savings account or into a retirement plan or an investment account.

Tithers who are believing for God's increase in their lives are looking down the road to the "better life" that God has for them. They aren't expecting God to pull a divine dump truck up to their driveway and unload several tons of gold coins. No! They are expecting God to provide for them "good deals," "wise investments," "smart choices," and "prime opportunities." They are partners with God in the growth of their lives, their bank accounts, their real estate holdings, and their investment portfolios.

Why Do Tithers Exhibit These Traits? Why do I see these three trends in tithers more than in non-tithers? I believe the main reason is not that people are more careful with less money than more money. People who are careless with money are careless with money no matter how much the amount. Just because ten percent is taken out of the realm of "personal spending" doesn't make a person more conscientious about spending.

No, the real reason is a faith issue. People who tithe start *expecting* God's blessing. They start *looking to God* for the total management of their lives. They start expecting God to change *everything* about them. They start seeing a better neighborhood in which to raise their children and a better school for their children to attend. They start seeing a better job that is more fulfilling and uses more of their talents. They start seeing a better education for themselves, whether it's going back to college or getting a specific skill in a specialty course. They start envisioning a better use of their time, which usually means getting involved in a ministry outreach that truly gives them a purpose for living.

When you are trusting God for a better life, you see yourself as a partner in making that life happen. You want to put yourself in the best possible position for God to use you, raise you up, and bless you. Life becomes more focused, less scattered. And with that, there's a greater focus on financial matters. There's less "throwing money to the wind" and more care about how to *focus* spending and

God's Way Works!

"**M**y own testimony is miraculous. I personally know that there is power in the seed you plant. At one point in my life I was so broke that I lived in the basement of my parents' house and did not even have a car. I had lost everything. It was mentally tough to bounce back from such huge losses. I had to fight my circumstances with the Word. In other words, I had to speak with my mouth what God said about me, even though circumstances denied it all. (See Romans 4:17.)

"I told myself I would recover. I preached to myself that I would get back all that I had lost.

"At my lowest point, God spoke to my heart and told me to give my way out of trouble. I soon had an opportunity to give the very last money I had for missionary work. I gave the money, and I have been blessed ever since that time. It sill amazes me how God turned everything around in my life. If He did it for me, He will do it for you!" — Bishop Dennis Leonard investing in ways that will bring about a *better* return or that will purchase a truly *better* quality of life.

Tithing will change the way you think about money. It will make you *want* to become more disciplined.

In the end, those who tithe find that the ninety percent that is theirs to spend in any godly, moral, ethical way they choose to spend it will *go further* and *accomplish more*. It's ninety percent that has God's favor on it. It will do more than a hundred percent that doesn't have God's favor on it!

Essential #3: Determination

Determination is a third quality that is necessary for genuine change to occur in your life. It can be summed up in two words: work and perseverance.

How do you spell "success"? W-O-R-K. Success doesn't fall out of the sky and hit you on the head. Success comes only with diligence and hard work. Diligent people always put in more time than is required of them. They go to work early, stay late, and don't procrastinate. They don't put everything off until tomorrow or until they "feel" like it. They get up and get busy.

Tithing isn't an excuse for not working. To the contrary, those who tithe are excited about working. They are eager to work. They are getting ready for God's blessing and they know work is part of that blessing.

Have you ever met a person who says, "I'm looking forward to retiring so I can do what I want to do"?

Have you ever known a person who lives for the weekend—a person who says, "I can hardly wait for the weekend to come so I can do what I want to do"?

My advice to people who say things like this is: Start doing what you want to do right now! The person who lives for retirement or lives for the weekend is a person who is locked into a job he doesn't enjoy. Get into a job that you truly love doing and give your creativity, energy, and time to doing that job to the best of your ability!

The second aspect of determination is perseverance. If you truly want any change to occur in your life, you have to stick with the discipline you've adopted long enough for the change to take place.

A truck driver once said to me, "If you're barreling down the highway in an eighteen-wheeler at seventy miles an hour and you suddenly realize that you should be going the opposite direction, it takes a little while to make the U-turn."

The same is true in life. If you want a one-hundred-and-eighty-degree turnaround in your life on any front, the process is going to take a little time.

Don't shortchange yourself by saying, "God didn't move things for me." You just didn't have patience to see things move!

It might take you several months to get all those credit cards paid off—if you've dug yourself into a deep credit-card hole it might even take you a couple of years to pay off that debt. It might take you some time to save up what you need for a down payment on a house of your own. It might take you some time to get the training you need so you can qualify for a better job or start on the career that you've desired to have all along.

Part of determination is persevering. It's enduring. It's sticking with the plan. It's refusing to give up.

The plan *starts* with tithing. Tithing starts the blessing process. Tithing isn't a one-time thing. A blessing isn't a one-time thing. There's a rhythm that needs to be established.

Tithing is giving ten percent from your paycheck this week...and then ten percent from your paycheck next week...and then ten percent from your paycheck the next week...and on and on and on. For how long? Well...how long do you want God's blessing?

Blessing is receiving from God today...and tomorrow...and the next day...and the next and the next and the next and the next.

Remember what I said earlier. It's a cycle. It's believing...giving to God...receiving God's blessings...believing...giving to God...receiving God's blessings...and on and on and on.

If you need to acquire a new desire...

If you need to acquire more discipline...

If you need to renew your determination and acquire a new level of energy for your work...

Fast and pray about what you need. Ask God to give you His desire, to help you acquire and maintain the right disciplines in your life, and to renew your ability to work hard and persevere in the tasks you under-take.

Begin to speak God's Word to your life and to your situation. There's power in God's Word. Let the words you speak energize and activate your faith.

Stay consistent in your giving. Give your tithe. Give offerings. As you do, release your faith, trusting God to activate His supernatural cycle of blessing in your life!

MAKE A COMMITMENT:

"I will make God's desires my desires.

I will discipline myself. I will work and persevere

with determination to live the way God commands."

Visit online at www.dennisleonardministries.com.

17

FIGHT THE GOOD FIGHT

A man once said, "The only *good* fight is the fight you *win*." I truly believe that and I believe the Bible teaches that. When God tells us to fight the good fight of faith, He intends for us to *win!* (See 1 Timothy 6:12.)

The fact is, we do have "fights" in this life—not with other people, but with the devil and his host of demons. We fight against disease, oppression, discouragement, fear, anger, and a host of temptations. The fight of faith is the fight of *life*.

God never promises us a life with no problems. He does promise to help us fight and win, and as we obey Him and trust Him and give to Him, He promises us a life of blessings. Along with blessings come "persecutions."

As much as I believe that God's desire is to prosper you and to move you into a life of abundance and financial freedom, I also know that when God starts blessing you, the enemy of your soul is likely to increase conflict and troubles in your life. The last thing the devil wants to see is your salvation, your prosperity, or your wholeness.

Loving the Lord doesn't mean "living on easy street." Every believer faces times of trouble, trial, and difficulty. No matter who the person is, he is subject to lost finances, family breakups, job crises, and disasters all around.

Why?

First, we live in a fallen world that is dominated by sin and evil.

Second, we live in relationship with other people and the will of other people around us may not be in line with God's commandments and principles.

You do not live in a vacuum. What other people do is related to your finances. Your spouse can make choices that destroy your marriage quite apart from your desire to serve God and obey Him in all things. Your children have wills of their own and they can make choices that are devastating in spite of all you do to protect them, warn them, advise them, and pray for them. Your employer can make decisions that fly in the face of your good job performance and loyalty. No person is immune from the sin, failures, and errors made by other people.

The good news is also two-fold.

First, God promises to be *with* you in your time of difficulty.

Second, God promises to *deliver* you from a time of trial.

Read God's Word and believe it:

- *"Many are the afflictions of the righteous: but the LORD delivereth him out of them all"* (Psalm 34:19). God is always in the delivering business!

- *"The LORD redeemeth the soul of his servants: and none of them that trust in him shall be desolate"* (Psalm 34:22). A believer may feel abandoned and suffer loss but he will never be left desolate or alone. No matter what the devil throws at you, he cannot destroy your relationship with God or capture your eternal soul!

- *"Weeping may endure for a night, but joy cometh in the morning"* (Psalm 30:5). Believers in Christ Jesus are not spared sorrow in this life, but the joy of the Lord always prevails.

Fight the Good Fight

God's Challenge to Us. God's challenge to us in hard times is to keep believing in Him, keep trusting Him, keep obeying Him, and keep looking for the Lord to turn things around on your behalf. The psalmist said, *"Be of good courage, and he shall strengthen your heart, all ye that hope in the LORD"* (Psalm 31:24).

Choose to believe for the good thing that God has promised. Believe in His promise more than you believe the neighborhood gossip, the economic reports on television, or the advice of an ungodly counselor. Don't call in to a radio program for your answers. Go to the Word of God and trust God to give you *His* answer, which is an answer you can stake your future on and take with you all the way to the finish line of your life!

You may be broke today...but that doesn't mean you'll be broke forever. Trust God! Believe for God to work His good thing in your life.

You may be going through a tough time today...but that doesn't mean all your life will be a tough time. Trust God! Believe for God to turn things around. Visit online at www.dennisleonardministries.com.

You may have had a setback...get ready for a comeback!

Trust God to prove the truth of Romans 8:28 in your life: *"We know that all things work together for good to them that love God, to them who are the called according to his purpose."* If you are saved, you are the *"called."* If you are saved, God has a purpose and a plan for your wholeness and prosperity. Trust God to work out *all* things for your good. Keep loving God. Keep trusting Him!

Hide God's Word in your heart and believe His Word no matter how bleak the situation, dark the day, or threatening the circumstances:

Remember ye not the former things, neither consider the things of old. Behold, I will do a new thing; now it shall spring forth; shall ye not know it? I will even make a way in the wilderness, and rivers in the desert (Isaiah 43:18–19).

- *A Sure Way.* Note that this verse says God will make a *way* in the wilderness. A desert wilderness is marked by shifting sands. In a desert, what may appear to be the "way" one day can disappear overnight. God promises to make a way that is sure, one you can count on, one that doesn't shift on you.

- *A River of Life.* Note that God promises refreshment in the midst of everything that is unrefreshing. A desert is marked by a lack of water. That can mean a lack of spiritual refreshment, a lack of energy and vitality, a lack of hope and dreams, a lack of creativity and enthusiasm. God promises to give you a life that is marked by a *river* of spiritual refreshment. It's a river of life, of dreams and desires fulfilled, of new ideas and fresh enthusiasm.

Trust God to do His "new thing" in your life!

We Must Fight for the Blessing. God responds to those who are willing to fight in the spiritual realm for what they desire and what is rightfully theirs. God is looking for people who are determined to follow Him, even if it means spiritual battle with the enemy of their souls. The devil is defeated when a person stands up in Christ and declares, "I'm serving God with all that I am and all that I have." The apostle Paul called this *"the good fight of faith"* (1 Timothy 6:12).

If you will make up your mind to fight for your blessings by giving...by praying...by putting God first...the devil cannot stop your harvest from coming.

Always keep in mind that you are in a spiritual war. You will win if you stand your ground and remain faithful.

It isn't just the devil that fights you on giving. Your own fleshly desires also will rise up in you. There will be that little voice inside your mind that says, "Don't give. Wouldn't you rather have...?" When you hear that voice, fight back by giving *extra!*

Make up your mind to win. Be determined to gain the victory. You are anointed by God for blessing, but you have to fight back the forces of evil and the forces of your own fleshly desire to have it.

Why Does the Devil Fight You So Hard?

There are two main reasons the devil fights you so hard. The first reason is very simple: It's the devil's nature to fight you. Jesus said the devil is a liar and a thief by nature. He only comes to steal from us, destroy us, and kill us. (See John 10:10.)

Fight the Good Fight

Do you know the story of the turtle and the scorpion? A scorpion wanted to get across the river so he asked the turtle for a ride. "No way," replied the turtle. "If I give you a ride, you will sting me and kill me."

The scorpion said, "I won't sting you. If I did, I might drown. I promise I won't hurt you." That seemed to make a little sense to the turtle so it said, "Well, okay. Climb on my back, and I'll give you a ride across the river."

The turtle began to swim across the river with the scorpion on its back. Then, as they neared the opposite shore, the scorpion suddenly stung the turtle. As the turtle lay dying on the bank, he gasped, "You lied to me. You told me you wouldn't hurt me. Why did you sting me?"

The scorpion laughed, "You stupid fool. Don't you know that stinging is what I do? I stung you because it is my nature to sting. I can't help myself."

That's the way the devil works in our lives. He will promise us all sorts of things that we desire or perceive to be good. But there's always a "sting" in what the devil gives to us. It is the devil's nature to lie, deceive, steal, kill, and destroy.

The Devil Hates the Possibility of Your Success. The second reason the devil fights so hard is because the person who believes God, obeys God, and gives to God's work is a person who is going somewhere. The devil doesn't want you to succeed because your

God's Way Works!

"I am only nineteen years old but I had a need. I had never seemed to be able to meet a nice guy to date and get to know. I have met many who were not what they proclaimed to be, and I was becoming frustrated. In church one Sunday, Bishop Leonard said to plant your biggest seed and ask God for something. I gave all I had, which was a hundred dollars. I prayed and asked God to send me a godly boyfriend. As unbelievable as it seems, within a few weeks I met a guy who is better than I could have imagined. He is a real man of God. Truly God is concerned about everything in our lives!" — Amanda

147

success brings glory to God. Your success enables you to fund ministries and to do things that aren't presently being done to extend the kingdom of God. Your success gives the devil a black eye.

The devil will do his best to lower your expectations. God does everything to raise your expectations. He wants you to believe in Him and to trust Him for better health, better finances, a better career, and complete restoration of all that has been taken from you in the past. The word of the Lord is for people who want more than they have. It is not just about money or prosperity. It is about health, peace, joy, spiritual authority, and effectiveness in winning souls. The word of the Lord is for people who aren't content to live in the future the way they have lived in the past—it's for people who want more of God and who want to have more influence for God. The word of the Lord is about increase, not decrease or maintaining the status quo. It's about moving forward, upward, and onward.

The devil will tell you that you are always going to live on "Barely Get Along Street." Tell the devil you're packing your bags and getting ready to move to "Abundance Avenue"!

The devil will tell you that other people are always going to keep you down. Tell the devil that you are trusting God to lift you up!

Stop listening to the negative voices that try to keep you right where you are...that tell you the future is going to be just like the past...that tell you all that you can't do and can't become. Confess with your mouth that this is your time and that you're going to be blessed by God *this* year. Quit waiting for "someday" to show up. Start pursuing God's best for you *today!*

Negativity will eat up your energy. It will kill your faith. It will destroy any desire that you have for something better in your life.

The number one way to combat those negative voices that speak to you is to speak aloud the Word of God. Let the Word build your faith.

Then, stand your spiritual ground based upon the Word of God that you have spoken. Do you remember the story of Shammah? The Philistines had come up against the Israelites and on one particular day, the Philistine troops had gathered for a battle on a piece of ground that was full of lentils—in other words, it was a bean field.

Fight the Good Fight

All the Israelites fled from the Philistines, except one man. Shammah, who was one of the mighty men of David, stood in the midst of that field and defended it. He took on the Philistines single-handedly and defeated them, and the Bible tells us, *"The LORD wrought a great victory"* (2 Samuel 23:11–12).

Shammah refused to yield to the enemy the territory that belonged to God's people—even to the yielding of a bean field! So many times we give in the devil, telling ourselves or others, "Oh, that's just a little thing." The truth is, absolutely nothing that is good, beneficial, or godly should *ever* be conceded to the devil. He shouldn't have one dime, one ounce, one acre, one bit of *any* of the wealth that God has laid up for the righteous.

Stand your ground! Don't let the devil run over you.

Your Authority to Defeat the Devil. Do you have the authority to keep the devil from stealing from you? The Bible says you do. The Bible says that you can take the Word of God, which the apostle Paul called *"the sword of the Spirit,"* and by the power of the Holy Spirit and in the name of Jesus, you can defeat the devil's attacks against you. You can stop him from stealing your joy, stealing your future, stealing your family, stealing your *life.*

You have the power to pray.

I love the old proverb that says, "Worry over nothing and pray over everything." That's God's way.

You have the power to keep planting seeds and wrapping them with your faith.

Trust me on this, the devil *especially* doesn't want you to get a revelation about tithing. He knows that if you get under God's blessing and begin to experience God's favor, you will do more than you have ever done before to win souls and influence people for Christ. Success will be waiting for you around every corner, and the more you experience that success, the more you will desire to serve God.

I've seen it happen over and over—those who tithe also become more faithful in their church attendance and in their involvement in the various ministries and outreaches of their church. Those who tithe become more faithful in their prayer life—there's a freedom in their prayers because they know they are in total right standing with God. Their petitions are bolder, their intercessions stronger. They have a renewed desire to read the Word of God—they are eager to find all of God's promises related to their life, eager to know the words and work of Jesus, eager to experience the power of the Holy Spirit at work in them and through them, and eager to know all of God's commandments so they might obey them.

You have the power to outlast the down times and delays.

Even though a blessing may be delayed, it cannot be denied if you are walking with the Lord. At times the Lord delays a specific blessing because He knows the timing isn't right, or there may be something He desires for you to learn before you are able fully to handle His blessing. But the blessing *will* come.

Don't be discouraged if your breakthrough hasn't come yet.

Don't be impatient or let yourself fall into doubt and unbelief.

Stick with what God has empowered you to do! Keep doing it. Keep giving. Keep trusting God. It's only a matter of time until your harvest comes!

If you put money in the bank on a certificate of deposit, you have to leave it there for a certain amount of time or you won't receive any interest or increase on that deposit. If you get impatient and take out the money before the time, you will lose out on any interest you may have accumulated on the funds. The same is true in God's kingdom. Planting in the kingdom of God has seasons. You must wait for the right timing on the return. God alone knows when that due season is scheduled.

You may have some down moments, but ultimately you will succeed.

The great prophet Elijah killed eight hundred of God's enemies in a day, and the next day he was so depressed he wanted to die. Emotions are fickle. You can be up one day and down the next. That's why we must never live by our emotions. If our emotions rule us, they'll ruin us.

Life's circumstances can turn your emotions inside out if you left them. Feelings will fool you. They'll cause you to think things are good when they aren't, and to think things are terrible when they are actually improving. Don't trust your emotions. Trust God! Keep doing what He tells you to do. Keep believing in Him. God tells us in His Word, *"Many are the afflictions of the righteous: but the LORD delivereth him out of them all"* (Psalm 34:19).

You have the power to forget the past and press forward!

've met people who seem to need a memory transplant to enable them to forget their own past sins. They are continually harping on what they did or didn't do in the past. The truth of God's Word is that when you are forgiven by God, He forgets your sins. He casts them as far away from Himself as the east is from the west (Psalm 103:12). What God forgets, you need to forget!

Don't keep reminding yourself or God of things God has already forgotten.

Now, if you have never received God's forgiveness, you need to confess to Him that you are a sinner, that you are sorry for your sins, and that you want to receive Jesus as your Savior. If you have never done this, I invite you to pray today:

"Father, I admit to You that I'm a sinner. I've done things I know are displeasing to You and that have been against Your commandments. I am truly sorry. I accept Your only Son, Jesus Christ, as my Savior. I believe that He died on the cross for my sins so I could be forgiven and begin to walk in a new-ness of life. Help me to turn away from my old life and my old sins forever, and to trust You to lead me and guide me from this day on. Heal me and cleanse me of all that is my past. Make me a new person in You. Thank You for doing this. I ask it in the name of Jesus. Amen."

God's Word says that if you will pray a prayer like that and mean it from your heart, your sins *will* be forgiven. You then must choose to forgive yourself. Leave your sins behind and walk forward!

It's not God who reminds you of what happened to you in the past. It's the devil who reminds you of your past sins in a way that makes him an "accuser." The Bible refers to the devil as the *"accuser of our brethren...which accused them before our God day and night"* (Revelation 12:10).

Your own mind also can act like a broken record player that is stuck and continually seeks to replay the past over and over and over and over.

Turn off the broadcasts from the devil into your heart and turn off the broken record player in your own mind! Get ready to sing a new song of joy, a song of a fabulous future filled to overflowing with the blessings of God.

Pray Philippians 3:13–14 over your life:

Brethren, I count not myself to have apprehended: but this one thing I do, forgetting those things which are behind, and reaching forth unto those things which are before, I press toward the mark for the prize of the high calling of God in Christ Jesus.

Forget about the mistakes and sins of your past. Confess them to God...get His forgiveness...forgive yourself...and then press on! Focus your eyes on the future God has for you.

Abram was a moon worshiper until he heard the voice of God and began to put his faith in the one, true, and living Lord. The Lord changed Abram's name and he became Abraham, which means "father of many nations."

David was a shepherd boy out in a field. As the youngest son in the family, he had little future to anticipate. Then one day the prophet of God anointed him and, over time, he became a mighty king.

Ruth was a stranger in an adopted land, but she followed God and became part of the lineage of the Messiah.

What will God do for you if you put Him first in every area of your life? How far could you go? What blessings could you have?

It's time to forget the past and move into your future!

You have the power to *hope.*

Are you aware that human beings are the only creatures on this earth who have the ability to *hope?* Set your eyes on what lies ahead! Believe for it. Hope for it.

Fight the Good Fight

If we only knew what God has in store for us as His children! Our insight and imagination falls so short of *all* that He has for us!

Sometimes God works in a process. At other times, God works very quickly. The shackles that are binding a person can suddenly fall away. A person can be in the desert for forty years, but in one day be delivered. *Suddenly* things change for the better.

Suddenly, there's a call about a job.

Suddenly, you're approved for a new house.

Suddenly, you meet a person who introduces you to a person who introduces you to a person.

Suddenly, you feel energy and enthusiasm again.

Look for that suddenly moment. *Hope for it! Believe for it!* And then...don't miss it! If you continue to tolerate the bad that is around you, you may miss that new and sudden opportunity that God sends your way.

MAKE A COMMITMENT:
"I will keep fighting the devil until my harvest of blessing comes."

18

SACRIFICIAL OFFERINGS PRODUCE BREAKTHROUGHS

A re you in need of a real "breakthrough" in your finances? Do you feel as if there's a prison wall around you so that nothing of God's blessings seems to be able to penetrate it and enter into your life?

Jesus encountered a woman who no doubt felt this way. She lived in the time of the prophet Elisha.

Now there cried a certain woman of the wives of the sons of the prophets unto Elisha, saying, Thy servant my husband is dead; and thou knowest that thy servant did fear the LORD: and the creditor is come to take unto him my two sons to be bondmen. And Elisha said unto her, What shall I do for thee? tell me, what hast thou in the house? And she said, Thine handmaid hath not any thing in the house, save a pot of oil. Then he said, Go, borrow thee vessels abroad of all thy neighbours, even empty vessels; borrow not a few. And when thou art come in, thou shalt shut the door upon thee and upon thy sons, and shalt pour out into all those vessels, and thou shalt set aside that which is full. So she went from him, and shut the door upon her and upon her sons, who brought the vessels to her; and she poured out. And it came to pass, when the vessels were full, that she said unto her son, Bring me yet a vessel. And he said unto her, There is not a vessel more. And the oil stayed. Then she came and told the man of God. And he said, Go, sell the oil, and pay thy debt, and live thou and thy children of the rest (2 Kings 4:1–7).

This woman had a tremendous need in her life. Her sons were about to be taken from her to be slaves. In that time, slavery was an acceptable form of repaying a loan that couldn't be paid otherwise. For this woman, her sons represented *her* financial sustenance— after the death of her husband, they were her means of support. To lose her sons didn't just pay the debt; it utterly destroyed her future well-being. If anybody ever needed a financial breakthrough, this woman did.

She did the right thing. She went to the prophet of God to see what the Word of the Lord would be to her and her family.

Elisha asked her what she had in her possession. The only thing she had of value was a little jar of oil. He told her to start pouring out that oil into every vessel she could put her hands on.

In the natural, this was a total waste of the oil she had. But in the supernatural, the pouring out of her only bit of wealth was the "seed" that God could use to bring her a harvest.

She didn't just pour a little out of that small jar of oil. She poured...and she poured...and she poured. She filled every container she had as well as all those that her sons were able to borrow from neighbors. She didn't stop pouring until there were no vessels left. The sale of the oil was sufficient to pay the debt and give her a starting income until her sons could work.

This woman could have heard the advice from the prophet and responded, "That doesn't make sense. I'm not going to do that." Instead, she *believed* what the prophet told her. And then she *acted* on it.

Sacrificial Offerings Produce Breakthroughs

The Bible tells us that faith without works is *dead* (James 2:20). It's unproductive. It doesn't produce anything. But...faith coupled with works is *powerfully alive*. It produces. It yields blessing. It grows a harvest.

Sacrifice: Faith in Action

Christians today don't like to hear the word *sacrifice*. Certainly we aren't called to sacrifice today in the way the Israelites were commanded to sacrifice in the Old Testament. The sacrificial offering system of the Old Testament was completely fulfilled in the death of Jesus on the cross. He was the ultimate and final "blood sacrifice" for the forgiveness of sin. No more sacrifice of animals or birds was required.

Jesus' death on the cross, however, did not negate the system of giving of tithes. We still are required to tithe and give offerings as a mark of our obedience, faith, love, and trust.

Sacrificial giving is *still* in effect, just not with a blood sacrifice from animals.

Sacrifice means "cost." It is the giving of something that is highly valued. And most Christians today don't want to give up what they value highly. They prefer to live a life of self-fulfillment with bigger barns and greater resources, without any faith or sacrifice involved.

Money has always been one of the hardest things for people to give up. It's something valued, and valued highly. To give it, without receiving back anything tangible, goes against our human nature.

In the story of this woman who had a pot of oil, the oil was like money to her. To pour it out—to give it up—no doubt was hard. It took courage and faith for her to do it.

Sacrifice Throughout God's Word. Sacrifice is mentioned throughout the Bible. Read just a sample of what God's Word says:

- *"Then Jacob offered sacrifice upon the mount, and called his brethren to eat bread: and they did eat bread, and tarried all night in the mount"* (Genesis 31:54). We are to sacrifice *together* with others who believe and love God.

157

- *"Thou shalt therefore sacrifice the Passover unto the LORD thy God, of the flock and the herd, in the place which the LORD shall choose to place his name there"* (Deuteronomy 16:2). We are to make our sacrifice in the place of the Lord's choosing—the local church, His storehouse today.

- *"I will freely sacrifice unto thee: I will praise thy name, O LORD; for it is good"* (Psalm 54:6). We are to sacrifice *"freely"*—which means generously—and accompany our sacrifice with praise.

- *"I beseech you therefore, brethren, by the mercies of God, that ye present your bodies a living sacrifice, holy, acceptable unto God, which is your reasonable service"* (Romans 12:1). Sacrificial giving is a symbol of giving our total lives—it is our "reasonable service" to God!

What Is God Asking YOU to Sacrifice? What is God leading you to give to Him?

The priests in the Old Covenant never came before God empty-handed. They always brought a sacrificial offering when they came before Him. We, as God's *"kings and priests"* on this earth today, are to do the same. We are to come before Him with the gift of our lives and our substance—all that we are and all that we have. He promises, in return, to give us Himself—all that He is and all that He has.

Make your ongoing prayer, "Lord, what should I give next? What should I do next?" Faith is listening to God and then obeying what He says *He* wants to do in your life, for you and your family, and all around you!

A minister friend of mine felt led of the Lord to give away a beautiful car he owned. This wasn't easy for him. It was a great car. But he obeyed the Spirit of the Lord and believed for a blessing in return. Within a year that blessing came in the form of the house of his dreams. He said, "I gave a car and God gave me a house. He had a better idea than I had!"

Years ago God asked me to give away one of my most treasured possessions, a Harley Davidson motorcycle. That motorcycle had special meaning to me because it represented my reestablishing myself after a difficult time in my life. But I gave it, and I have never looked back.

The Sacrifice of Your "Offering"

The Hebrew word for gift is *mattan*. It means to bring a present to God. What do your gifts of God say about you? Are they generous gifts? Are they gifts from your heart?

For some people, the tithe can be an act of sacrifice from the heart. The tithe is commanded and "specified"—the firstfruits, ten percent. We give it in obedience.

An offering is commanded but not specified. It is *beyond* the tithe, beyond ten percent. It's "extra giving." We give it in a spirit of generosity and overflowing love, believing God for an overflowing blessing.

In many ways, your offering is an indication to the Lord of what you are believing you will receive from God in the future.

I had a man tell me one time about a preacher who told his congregation, "Whatever you give to God, I'm going to take it to God and say to Him, 'I guess this is their tithe and offering.' And then, I'm going to expect God to multiply that amount you've given by ten percent and make that your new income."

Several people in the church came up after the service and said, "Oh, preacher, don't do that!" He said, "Why not?"

One man said, "Well, I only put in ten dollars and if God takes that amount and multiplies it by ten, I'm only going to be making a hundred dollars a week. I can't live on that!"

God's Way Works!

"I sowed a seed into the service and ministry of Heritage Christian Center one night. You told us to write down the things we were believing God for, and I did. One of the things was for my husband to find a job here in the city and not have to go overseas to work. Today my husband has that job. He is making more than he did when he was away. I also wrote down that I want to have my own business. I know it is just a matter of time." — Mona

The preacher replied, "What is it that you *want* to live on?"

The man said, "I want to live on more than what I'm making now."

"Well, then," the preacher replied, "you should be giving the full tithe and the offering to the amount that, when it's multiplied by ten, you like the number!"

This man went home and wrote a check for eighty dollars. He was making seven hundred dollars a week, so his tithe was seventy dollars. He started believing God for eight hundred dollars a week, which would have been a tithe of eighty dollars. He made that extra ten dollars a week his "offering" in anticipation of the day it would one day be his tithe.

Are you curious about what happened? I was. I asked the man who told me this story and he smiled. He said, "I'm the guy. I'm making twelve hundred dollars a week now. My pay was increased to eight hundred dollars a week just four months after I started giving my tithe *and* an offering. That was two years ago. I'm giving more than my tithe every week because, Bishop, I'm still not at the top of what I *want* to earn."

He quickly added, "Or what I want to *give*." He went on to say, "I get more kick out of giving now than I ever did when I coughed up only a ten-dollar bill each Sunday. My goal is to one day *give* every week more than I was earning a week."

You do the math. He's got a way to go but he's got a *desire*. He's disciplined—not only in his giving, but in his spending—as never before. He's determined to make that goal. He's working hard. He's persevering.

Is this man prospering? Absolutely. And in more ways than in just his bank account.

Blessings Flow from Sacrifice

When I talk to people who are greatly blessed and I ask them to trace their wealth back to the beginning of their blessing, I nearly always hear a story of sacrifice. Even ungodly people who are materially or financially wealthy speak of sacrifice. Some tell how they sacrificed their time. Some tell how they sacrificed their life savings. Some tell how they sacrificed their success in one career to pursue the career they truly believed God had called and equipped them to have.

Sacrificial gifts have two distinct characteristics:

- *Sacrificial Gifts Are the Best Gift We Can Make.* God is worthy of your best—no leftovers, no tokens. He is worthy of your highest, first, and best gift!

- *A Sacrificial Gift "Costs"* **Something.** David refused to offer anything to God that did not cost him anything. When he bought the threshing floor in Jerusalem, the man who owned the floor said he would give it to David. David replied, *"Nay; but I will surely buy it of thee at a price: neither will I offer burnt offerings unto the LORD my God of that which doth cost me nothing. So David bought the threshingfloor and the oxen for fifty shekels of silver"* (2 Samuel 24:24).

What was the result of David's sacrifice? *"The plague was stayed from Israel"* (2 Samuel 24:25).

Why Make a Sacrificial Gift? Because sacrificial giving is an outward expression of an inward desire to sell out to God. It is a sign that we are putting *all* our faith and trust in the Lord. And in the spiritual realm, sacrificial giving kicks dirt in the devil's face and says, "No matter what, my faith and hope are in Jesus Christ!"

It is the sacrificial gift that is accepted by God as the generous gift. It is giving in *great* measure, with a desire to receive back a *great* measure of God's highest and best blessings.

When We Sacrifice, God Responds

Throughout the Bible God called His people to sacrifice, and God always responded with a blessing. Perhaps the greatest example of this is in the life of Abraham. He was called by God to take his son, Isaac, to a very specific mountain and to offer him up to God in a sacrifice. It was the most difficult test of Abraham's life.

Just at the precise moment when Abraham had his knife in his hand, ready to kill Isaac—and believing all the time for God to raise him back up from the dead—God provided a ram caught in the thorns of a nearby bush to replace Isaac. The word of the Lord came to Abraham very clearly and Isaac's life was spared. (See Genesis 22:1–18.)

I want you to notice three things about this story.

First, Abraham obeyed. God told him what to do and Abraham *"rose up early in the morning"* and set out to do it. He didn't delay in following God's command. He didn't make any excuses or embark on any "delay tactics."

Second, Abraham believed God would make a way. The Bible says when Isaac asked about the sacrifice, Abraham said, *"My son, God will provide himself a lamb for a burnt offering"* (Genesis 22:7). In Hebrews, we read that Abraham believed about Isaac that *"God was able to raise him up, even from the dead"* (Hebrews 11:19). Abraham didn't fully *want* to make this sacrifice, but he believed God would provide for him as he made the sacrifice.

Third, Abraham called the name of the place where the sacrifice took place, *"Jehovah-jireh"*—which means "God who provides." He knew the provision of the lamb was from the Lord.

This is the same pattern we are to follow in our tithing:

God's Way Works!

"**A**fter hearing this teaching on sacrificial giving, I decided I was going to test God. While I wrote out a check for the church offering, I told God that I still had to feed my family and put gas in the car for the next two weeks. I was sacrificing for Him to show me He is real. After church I was very nervous. I only had forty-five dollars to my name. I went to the grocery store and everything on my list was on sale or 'buy one, get one free'! I somehow left the grocery store with more than I had planned to buy, yet I still had money to put gas in the car. I was amazed also that in that two-week period I did not get any unexpected requests to pay for anything at the kids' school or anywhere else. My parents, who did not know about my sacrifice, had us over for dinner at least twice during that time, which helped us make it through. God made me believe that He has made a way for me, even when I doubted Him." — Shaquanda

Sacrificial Offerings Produce Breakthroughs

- We are to obey God.

- We are to believe God will make a way for *all* our needs to be met.

- We are to respond with praise after we make our sacrifice because we are *anticipating* the blessing that is coming from God's hand.

What was God's response to Abraham's sacrificial giving? Just read it!

Because thou hast done this thing...in blessing I will bless thee, and in multiplying I will multiply thy seed as the stars of the heaven, and as the sand which is upon the sea shore; and thy seed shall possess the gate of his enemies; and in thy seed shall all the nations of the earth be blessed; because thou hast obeyed my voice (Genesis 22:16–18).

This is also the message of the New Testament. The apostle Paul wrote to the Corinthians:

But this I say, He which soweth sparingly shall reap also sparingly; and he which soweth bountifully shall reap also bountifully. Every man according as he purposeth in his heart, so let him give; not grudgingly, or of necessity: for God loveth a cheerful giver. And God is able to make all grace abound toward you; that ye, always having all sufficiency in all things, may abound to every good work (2 Corinthians 9:6–8).

God delights in superlatives. Notice these phrases in the passage above:

- Reap *"bountifully."* God wants a person who sows bountifully to *reap* bountifully—that's a harvest of abundance!

- *"All grace abound."* God's work in every area of our life is to be experienced in a way that is described as "abounding." If you look up the word *abound* in a dictionary you are likely to find such phrases as these: great in number or amount...a large number or amount...fully supplied or filled...overflowing.

163

- *"All sufficiency in all things."* To experience sufficiency is to have enough of everything you need to do *"every good work"*—and to do every good work in a way that is also described as "abounding."

There's nothing lacking when we experience God's bountiful harvest in our lives. If we truly grasp that concept, we won't have any difficulty becoming a cheerful giver. We'll give with an I-can-hardly-wait, I'm-exited-and-overjoyed attitude!

If you are willing to pay the price and make the sacrifice today, God's favor will come upon you.

Accompany Your Sacrifice with Praise

God's Word calls us to a sacrifice of praise to accompany our sacrifices of giving: *"By him therefore let us offer the sacrifice of praise to God continually, that is, the fruit of our lips giving thanks to his name"* (Hebrews 13:15).

Praise doesn't happen automatically in our lives. We must *choose* to praise God. It isn't always easy to praise God as we put our tithe into the offering plate. We must *choose* to praise God. Praise is an act of love for God...it is an act of obedience...it is an act of faith!

God's Word tells us:

- *"Enter into his gates with thanksgiving, and into his courts with praise: be thankful unto him, and bless his name"* (Psalm 100:4).

- *"O give thanks unto the LORD; for he is good: because his mercy endureth for ever"* (Psalm 118:1).

- *"Let them shout for joy, and be glad, that favour my righteous cause: yea, let them say continually. Let the LORD be magnified, which hath pleasure in the prosperity of his servant"* (Psalm 35:27).

- *"For the LORD God is a sun and shield: the LORD will give grace and glory: no good thing will he withhold from them that walk uprightly"* (Psalm 84:11).

164

Sacrificial Offerings Produce Breakthroughs

Come before the Lord with praise on your lips, even as you voice with your faith the harvest you are expecting from God:

"God, I am so glad You saved me! I want to bring You a sacrificial gift to say thank You for all You've done. You have been so good to me. Lord, I know that You are concerned about all that concerns me, and I have some trouble in my life. I am giving you my sacrificial gift as a sign that I am giving *all* of myself to you. I am believing for You to deliver me and to give me all I need. Thank You, God, for I know that You have great plans for me. I receive those plans into my life starting *right now*. In Jesus' name I pray, amen."

Make Sacrificial Giving a Lifestyle

As you routinely begin to make sacrificial gifts to the Lord, this type of giving will become a lifestyle to you. Contrary to what the world may think or say, sacrificial giving becomes something that takes root deep inside you and brings you *joy*. The world sees giving as something painful, hurtful, and depressing. The Christian who gives the tithe with love and faith experiences *joy* at the coming harvest. As you give, think about the goodness and greatness of God that is opening up to you!

MAKE A COMMITMENT:
"I will make sacrificial offerings and give them with joy and praise to God!"

Visit online at www.dennisleonardministries.com.

19

THE POWER TO CREATE WEALTH

If you mention the word *wealth*, you get the attention of every person who hears your voice!

People in our world today routinely pack out seminars, conferences, and meetings in hotels that promise the information or means necessary to acquire wealth. People spend a great percentage of their time, and spend almost all of their talents and skills, on a quest for greater wealth. Some people sacrifice their health to get money...and then find that they have to spend that money in an attempt to regain their health!

As far as I am concerned, if you have enough money to pay your bills and have some left over to invest and have a vacation occasionally, you are living a blessed life!

If you are barely scraping by, living from week to week and paycheck to paycheck, with nothing left over...you need a breakthrough. You especially need a breakthrough in your thinking and believing.

If you believe that giving results in your having *less*, then you are into what I call a "poverty mentality." A poverty mentality sees money given as a loss rather than as an *investment*. A prosperity mentality looks ahead to the wealth that is going to be produced from what is given. A prosperity mentality anticipates that a person will receive *more* of what he invests. Start thinking "wealth" instead of "debt."

Start Wanting What God Wants

How wealthy does God want you to be? Here's what the Bible says: *"Beloved, I wish above all things that thou mayest prosper and be in health, even as thy soul prospereth"* (3 John 2).

God wants you healthy in your physical health and wealthy in your material possessions. He wants these things for you *"as thy soul prospereth"*—in other words, in direct proportion to your relationship with Him. The truth is, it is *as you trust God* with what you have, that *God entrusts you* with what He has—and all health, all material goods, and all spiritual peace and joy are His possessions!

We are called by God to start wanting what He wants...to start trusting Him and obeying Him...right where we are. Jesus told a parable about this:

> *For the kingdom of heaven is as a man travelling into a far country, who called his own servants, and delivered unto them his goods. And unto one he gave five talents, to another two, and to another one; to every man according to his several ability; and straightway took his journey. Then he that had received the five talents went and traded with the same, and made them other five talents. And likewise he that had received two, he also gained other two. But he that had received one went and digged in the earth, and hid his lord's money. After a long time the lord of those servants cometh, and reckoneth with them. And so he that had received five talents came and brought other five talents, saying, "Lord, thou deliveredst unto me five talents: behold, I have gained beside them five talents more. His lord said unto him, Well done, thou good and faithful servant: thou hast been faithful over a few things, I will make thee ruler over many things: enter thou into the joy of thy lord. He also that had received*

two talents came and said, Lord, thou deliveredst unto me two talents: behold, I have gained two other talents beside them. His lord said unto him, Well done, good and faithful servant; thou hast been faithful over a few things, I will make thee ruler over many things: enter thou into the joy of thy lord. Then he which had received the one talent came and said, Lord, I knew thee that thou art an hard man, reaping where thou hast not sown, and gathering where thou hast not strawed: and I was afraid, and went and hid thy talent in the earth: lo, there thou hast that is thine. His lord answered and said unto him, Thou wicked and slothful servant, thou knewest that I reap where I sowed not, and gather where I have not strawed: thou oughtest therefore to have put my money to the exchangers, and then at my coming I should have received mine own with usury. Take therefore the talent from him, and give it unto him which hath ten talents. For unto every one that hath shall be given, and he shall have abundance: but from him that hath not shall be taken away even that which he hath. And cast ye the unprofitable servant into outer darkness: there shall be weeping and gnashing of teeth (Matthew 25:14–30).

This parable teaches us clearly that if you can't trust God with a little bit of money, God won't trust you with more. If you can't trust God in little jobs, God won't trust you with big ones. If you have difficulty managing a hundred dollars, God isn't going to trust you with a million dollars.

Take a look at your ability to manage money. Take a look at your credit card debt. Take a look at your tithing. Would *you* trust you with more? If they're honest with themselves, most people would have to say "no."

God calls those who spend more than they bring in "wicked servants." Get rid of your debt. Don't buy things you can't afford. Don't drive a car you can't afford. Don't get into a mortgage you can't pay. Control what you spend. You can't be trusted with more until you learn to manage what you have!

This parable also teaches us that if we are willing to trust God with what we have and we learn to manage it well, God gives a tremendous return. Each of the servants in Jesus' parable who "invested their talents" *doubled* the amount they were given. And, they received the blessing of authority from their master. He made it very clear they were going to be given more to manage!

The apostle Paul wrote to Timothy about those who are chosen for spiritual leadership. He said, *"Moreover it is required in stewards, that a man be fond faithful"* (1 Corinthians 4:2). The point is, if a person is faithful in giving, he is nearly always faithful in his love for God and faithful in his relationships with people. Faithfulness in giving readily translates into faithfulness in relationships.

Faithful or Unfaithful Steward? Are you a faithful or an unfaithful steward of the resources and money God has put in your hands? Let me give you some very practical examples of what it means to be faithful and unfaithful in the stewardship of your money.

God's Word says to tithe. The faithful are those who tithe. The unfaithful are those who don't.

God's Word says to *"owe no man"* anything but godly love. The faithful pay their bills. The unfaithful are in continual deficit.

God's Word says that those who borrow money are slaves to their lenders. The faithful seek to get out of debt and refuse to buy on "credit" unless they can pay that bill in thirty days. The unfaithful stack up debt until they're drowning in it.

God's Word says to trust Him for wisdom in how to manage your money. The faithful learn principles of good money management from God's Word and use them. The unfaithful don't.

Let me ask you again:

Can God trust you?

Is tithing at the *top* of your budget?

Is your tithe the *first* check your write when you get paid?

Are You Trusting God to Help You Get Free of Debt? God will help you walk through the steps from debt to prosperity: Start by paying off your credit cards and clearing up your credit report. Then with the money you've freed up from credit card payments, start putting together the down payment on a home of your own. After

170

you get your house, start investing that money you had been saving each month toward the house down payment. Trust God to show you how to increase the return on your investments.

I recommend that if you are a woman you read Proverbs 31 very carefully. This woman wasn't only righteous and a good wife; she also was an excellent businesswoman! She knew how to manage money. She knew how to plan ahead and get work done. She knew how to turn a profit.

Moving from "Making It" to "Being Wealthy"

You will never grow spiritually until you are stretched. You won't be what God wants you to be until you are pushed out of your comfort zone and take a risk with your faith to believe that God truly *will* do what He says He will do in His Word. That's faith! That's trusting God to be God in all things!

It's a stretch for many people to believe they can generate wealth. It's a stretch for many to believe they can leave something worth passing on to their children. Proverbs 13:22 says, *"A good man leaveth an inheritance to his children's children."* In other words, it is God's desire to bless you so you can leave an inheritance to your family—not only your children but also your grandchildren. Don't just leave your family a funeral bill—leave something of value! That's what God wants. Do you want what God wants?

There are two aspects of wealth that I believe God has for *all* His children:

1. *A Business of Your Own.* Give thought and prayer to starting your own business. Many people have the capability of starting and running their own business. It takes diligence, planning, and a willingness to rise up and do something with your life. It takes *refusing* to become frustrated or to quit if you experience small setbacks.

One woman once said, "But all I know how to do is clean. I work as a janitor for a fast-food place at the airport." Cleaning is a valuable service! Consider starting a cleaning business of your own! Be diligent at every job that comes your way—work hard at it, give your best effort. Before long, you may have to hire employees to help you do all the work that comes your way.

I once heard about a man who came home from military service exhausted and disillusioned with life. He finally said to himself, "Well, at least I know how to clean a pool." He started cleaning pools for his neighbors. The time outside in the sun, doing something he found relaxing, was healing for him. He began to work harder and harder at cleaning pools—he learned about the chemicals needed to keep a pool clean and sanitary, the right brushes and systems to use, and so forth. Before long, he was cleaning more pools than he could personally handle! He developed an outlet for selling pool supplies and brushes. He hired a person to help him...and then another person...and eventually five people. He had a successful business!

Ask God to show you what you can do...and then start doing it!

Say to yourself, "I've had it with failure! I'm moving on to prosperity!"

2. *Property Ownership.* I encourage you to set a goal of buying property. In many cases, rent and mortgage payments are about the same amount. Start saving for the down payment on property you can *own.* God's great promise to Abraham was two-fold: land and children. It was God's blessing to Abraham and it's our blessing today as the "faith" heirs of Abraham.

Some people have their houses and their cars backward. They are driving expensive cars and living in apartments. Seek to own a home and leave the expensive car for later.

The minute you drive a new car off the lot, it loses ten to fifteen percent of its value! Cars depreciate rapidly in value. Houses, on the other hand, tend to increase in value over time.

As you become more experienced in handling finances, you may be able to shorten the length of your mortgage—perhaps from thirty to fifteen years. Your payment won't be that much more and you'll own your property sooner. Plus, you'll pay far less interest over time.

Get a plan! Start anticipating the property you'll purchase with the harvest God sends your way.

God has a "place for you to occupy." That means a place for you to "move into" and "own." God brought the children of Israel out of bondage in Egypt and led them to the Promised Land. He told them to "go up into the land and possess it" and that He would ensure their victory. God makes that same promise to us. He has a *place* for us that He desires for us to occupy. It's not only a place in the spiritual realm, but it's also a very real place on this earth. Everywhere you walk, you are to claim that territory for God. He has a place for you to dwell—in plain language, He has property He desires for you to own.

Under Joshua's leadership, the Israelites crossed the Jordan River and headed for the city of Jericho. Event though the city was a walled fortress, God provided a supernatural way for those walls to come tumbling down. God caused them to win despite the fortifications they faced. He'll do the same for you. He'll provide a way for you to purchase and occupy the place He has authorized for you.

The next city the Israelites confronted was Ai. It was such a small city that nobody gave it a second thought. A victory there seemed like an easy thing compared to Jericho. To the great surprise of the Israelites, the small and insignificant army of Ai defeated them. They asked God why this had happened. God replied, in effect, "Don't get mad at Me. There's disobedience in the camp. You've come under a curse." (See Joshua 7:11.)

What had happened? The Lord had instructed the Israelites not to take any of the goods or spoil from Jericho. As the first city conquered in the Promised Land, the spoil of Jericho was to be the "firstfruits" or the tithe. God's command had been, *"All the silver, and gold, and vessels of brass and iron, are consecrated unto the LORD: they shall come into the treasury of the LORD"* (Joshua 6:19).

A man named Achan had taken some of the spoil, however, and had hidden it and kept it as his private treasure. Nobody knew what he had done...except the one Person who mattered most. The Lord knew!

You may have a reputation as a pillar in your local church. People may see you as a great giver and a faithful follower of the Lord's commandments. God knows the *real* you. He is the one who truly knows if you are giving and faithfully following Him.

As a result of Achan's sin, trouble came upon the whole camp of Israelites. Achan caused the entire group to be defeated and thirty-six of his fellow Israelites to die in the battle.

Joshua cried out to God, the sin was revealed, and the people repented and obeyed God's commands. It was only after this sin was purged from the camp that the Israelites were able to go again and, this time, defeat Ai.

As you read through the book of Joshua about the conquest of the Promised Land, you'll find that the Israelites only got into trouble when there was sin in the camp. There's something about sin that stops faith and results in defeat. As long as the Israelites were walking in God's will, no enemy could stand against them. There's something about obedience that builds faith and results in victory!

God's Word says plainly, *"No weapon that is formed against thee shall prosper; and every tongue that shall rise against thee in judgment thou shalt condemn. This is the heritage of the servants of the LORD, and their righteousness is of me, saith the LORD"* (Isaiah 54:17). What a tremendous promise of God this is! But notice that this promise is the heritage of the *"servants of the LORD."* It is a promise to those who are serving the Lord, which means those who are keeping His commandments and pursuing His will with all their heart, soul, mind, and strength.

Trust God to Give You "Prosper Power"

Once you get into the rhythm of giving and reaping, obeying God, and putting Him first, God gives the power to create wealth. He doesn't just give money—for example, in the form of a gift or a job. He gives the *ability to make money.* He gives the energy to do a *good* job, ideas about how to be more effective and efficient in your work, creativity to come up with new products and procedures, and ideas about new services and new businesses.

When you make God your priority, He imparts favor on your job. You may start to realize opportunities coming from nowhere.

Wealth, of course, is far more than money and material goods. It's knowledge—not only knowledge about how to increase your income but also how to use your money properly and make it grow.

Personally, I don't worry or have concern about money. I can lose everything I have or give away everything I have because I know God has given me the ability to create wealth. If I lost it all or gave it all...I would get it all back...and more. Why do I have that confidence? Because I know how to give to God and trust Him.

A thief can steal money or material goods, but he cannot steal true wealth. True wealth lies in knowing Christ and knowing where you're headed in life and in eternity. True wealth is knowing that Christ is the source of all things that truly matter.

On June 1, 1902, a man by the name of Kerr—who lived in San Francisco—decided to put God to the test regarding this matter of tithing. He began tithing his income. After three months of tithing, he took a portion of the ninety percent he had remaining and started a company known as the Kerr Glass Company. He invested all that he owned into the company, which was a glass manufacturing company. Even though he had quite a bit of debt, he continued to tithe.

In 1906, a great earthquake demolished San Francisco. Just about every building in the San Francisco area was demolished or damaged...except Kerr's glass factory. Buildings on all sides of the factory were burned to the ground. The fire even scorched the wooden fence surrounding his property, but his factory was spared.

Are you trusting God today to surround your life in such a way that nothing about you can be touched by the devil, including your finances?

Not only can God *keep* you from experiencing a downturn, He can cause you to receive a sovereign, totally awesome *upturn*. Never lose sight of the fact that all the gold and silver belong to the Lord. So do the cattle on a thousand hills. God governs the living creatures, all forces of nature, and all mineral wealth! (See Psalm 50:10 and Haggai 2:8.) God's Word declares: *"But as it is written, Eye hath not seen, nor ear heard, neither have entered into the heart of man, the things which God hath prepared for them that love him"* (1 Corinthians 2:9).

God's Strategy for the End Times

I truly believe these next years will produce a harvest of souls for Jesus unlike anything that has ever been seen before. There will be people called to make some serious sacrifices...but I also believe we are going to see God give a thousand-fold return on those sacrifices!

The tremendous revival that will bring the saving of souls will occur simultaneously with God prospering His people. In fact, it's our prospering as His people that will "fund" the revival. It's the revival and saving of souls that will bring a massive outpouring of blessing to those who give.

God's promise to His people is that He will cause the devil to restore all that the devil has stolen (Joel 2:25). A great transference of wealth will go to the hands of the righteous, those who are truly in right standing with God and who are obeying Him. God is not going to place the wealth of the world into the hands of those He can't trust.

Don't miss out on what God has ahead!

Ask yourself today, "Can God trust me with money?" There are some Christians who can't handle money. If somebody handed them a million dollars, they would be using it in sinful ways before the month was out.

Are you learning God's ways for dealing with finances? Are you learning more about God and trusting Him to free you from depression, sickness, anger, and other things that motivate you to behave in ungodly ways? Are you walking in love, peace, joy, and forgiveness? Is your soul prospering?

The prospering of your *soul* is the first step toward the prospering of your entire life!

There is a shifting of things in the spiritual realm all around the world. Stop for a moment to consider all that has happened in just the last thirty or so years.

The Gospel is now preached in all nations. Jesus said this would happen in the last days (Mark 13:10). Christian television programs are being broadcast in areas that have never heard the Gospel before. We are closer to the end than you may think.

Communism has fallen in almost all areas of the world. The Berlin Wall came down in a day. When God says, "It's time!" things happen very quickly.

The governments of the world more and more are looking to the church to accomplish what the government has not been able to do. We see this in everything from prisons to welfare programs to drug rehab programs.

God has a hidden wealth in secret places set aside for these last days. Words can't express *all* that God is getting ready to do in the lives of those who will put Him first and choose to live their lives in accordance with His commandments. Clearly God is looking for people He can trust to use this hidden wealth to reach the world with the Gospel and show people how to live righteous lives.

MAKE A COMMITMENT:

"I'm going to get into the flow of God's highest and best blessings. I'm not going to miss out on *all* God desires to give me. I'm going to be a key player in God's end-time strategy!"

20

ENTER INTO FINANCIAL FREEDOM!

The ancient Israelites were slaves for more than four hundred years...but God delivered them in one night.

Joseph was in bondage as a slave and then in prison under false accusation and sentencing...but God delivered him in one day and promoted him to prime minister of the nation.

Daniel went from a lion's den to holding the second highest office in the Babylonian empire.

Don't underestimate what God can do.

Don't underestimate how quickly God can act!

Be ready to move when God does! Don't wait until tomorrow to start doing things God's way.

Don't rely on somebody else to do what only you can do. A change in your life is not up to your boss. It's not up to your spouse. It's not up to your pastor. It's up to *you*.

You are the one who has to decide that you are going to start doing things God's way...regardless of circumstances, regardless of what the world says.

You are the one who has to put God first in your life.

You are the one who has to obey the Lord in all things.

You are the one who has to bring the Lord your tithe and offerings.

You are the one who has to come to grips with your financial situation, set goals, make a budget and live within it, take control of your spending, make wise purchases, and develop good work habits.

You are the one who has to put away the idols in your life and lay aside the weight of all sin. Your flesh will always try to fight the will of God and take the opposite direction of a blessing. Choose God's way! You are the one who has to repent of sin and move into full surrender to the Lord. Read and heed God's Word:

Therefore also now, saith the LORD, Turn ye even to me with all your heart, and with fasting, and with weeping, and with mourning: and rend your heart, and not your garments, and turn unto the LORD your God: for he is gracious and merciful, slow to anger, and of great kindness, and repenteth him of the evil (Joel 2:12–13).

And what did the Lord say He would do on behalf of those who would do this? Read and be encouraged!

Be glad and rejoice: for the LORD will do great things...he hath given you the former rain moderately, and he will cause to come down for you the rain, the former rain, and the latter rain in the fist month. And the floors shall be full of wheat, and the fats shall overflow with wine and oil. And I will restore to you the years that the locust hath eaten, the cankerworm, and the caterpillar, and the palmerworm.... And ye shall eat in plenty, and be satisfied, and praise the name of the LORD your God, that hath dealt wondrously with you: and my people shall never be ashamed (Joel 2:21–26).

180

Enter into Financial Freedom!

You are the one who must activate your faith when you give and believe God for a full restoration of all the devil has stolen from you. You are the one who must use your faith to expect a *full* harvest in your *whole* life from the seeds you plant into God's work.

You are the one who must fill your heart with love and forgive those who have wronged you so you can walk in freedom and joy toward the blessings God has for you.

You are the one who must make God's desires your desires, discipline your life, and persevere in determination that you will *not* be denied the blessings God has ordained for your life and the life of your loved ones.

You are the one who has to fight the good fight against the devil and lay claim to all your blessings.

You are the one who must decide and then give sacrificial offerings—the kind that produce real breakthrough.

You are the one who must choose to pursue *wealth* and to use that wealth to win souls and expand God's kingdom.

In the end, you are the one who decides if you will enter into true financial freedom. The choices are yours to make.

I encourage you today—God has a strategy that works, not just for the person next to you but for *you*. His strategy is eternal, it's abundant, it's for you. Move into God's strategy...and you'll move into blessing!

MAKE A COMMITMENT:
"I will make the choices that lead me into financial freedom!"

Visit online at www.dennisleonardministries.com.